MY WAY
AN AUTOBIOGRAPHY
RUTH REESE

First published in 1985 by Gylendal Norsk Forlag, Oslo, Norway.

Published in Great Britain 1987 by

**Akira Press Ltd
307 Bethnal Green Road
London E2 6AH**

Printed and bound in Great Britain by
Anchor Brendon Ltd, Tiptree, Essex
All Rights Reserved
© 1985, 1987 Ruth Reese

British Library Cataloguing in Publication Data

Reese, Ruth
My Way: a life in music
1. Reese, Ruth 2. Afro-American musicians
—Biography
I. Title II. Min Vei. English
780'.92'4 ML 410.R24
ISBN 0-947638-21-0
ISBN 0-947638-22-9 pbk

Contents

This Book is Written in Memory of the Reese Clan,
WILLIAM
SARAH
CHARLEY
LULA
JACKSON
DOCK
HENRY
JOHN
LEON
ROSA
SARAH
SUSIE

PREFACE

To write ones autobiography is not Easy. It is difficult to write it without repeating that little pronoun,
"I" over and over. Some will say, perhaps, that I
praise myself too highly. What can I say to that? I
have written what happened. Why should I
subtract from what I have done simply to seem
humble.

My skin is black. I am descended from people
who were unwillingly brought to America, not
because they were loved or respected, but because
the southern plantation owners would get richer
by their coming. Having overlived the gruesome
passage from Africa's West Coast to the harbour
in America, shows the physical and psychological
strength they possessed. Many other died and were
thrown overboard to the sharks. Others willingly
hopped from the ship, thus becoming food for the
ocean inhabitants.

When they reached the American harbour, my
forefathers were placed on the auction block as
animals. If the buyer wanted to see them naked,
they were forced to comply. If the owner fancied a

young african girl purely for immoral purposes, no
one objected. He had his way. That was the black
African's first meeting with white civilisation. How
or why then can I be expected to feel a deep patriotism for a Nation that took even my name from
me, a Nation that gave my ancestors little chance
for developing as a people? (Yet, this same Nation
would like to bring their brand of democracy to old
cultures like Vietnam.) What the U.S.A. pays in
sending men to the moon and other excessive military spending is more than ample to pay for the
creation of jobs for the millions of people unemployed there. Take a good look around Chicago,
New York and every other town in America and
you will understand why there is such a high rate
of crime, narcotic mis-use and prostitution.

Well, I have shown where I stand. This business of
race is raised in almost every chapter in this book,
for no-where in the world am I allowed to think of
myself, for a single day, as just another human
being. I note with the exhibition of patriotism
shown by other people for their land. From the time
of their childhood, they are taught their nation's
history. They have their heroes, their monuments.
When they hear their National song, they take off
their hats and sing with gusto. That is impossible
for blacks in America when they hear the tunes,
"My Country 'Tis of Thee" and "The Star Span-
gled Banner". Yet, blacks have been in every war

fought by America. They fought against the British. They were on the side of Lincoln in the Civil War. As freed men and women, some went north seeking a better life, only to be met with hate and indifference. Some "good hearted" people and organisations tried to send them back to Africa to their homeland? Homeland? What homeland?

To feel proud of one's origin is very important to a thinking person. One must have this proudness rooted deep into ones consciousness. If not, one is insecure and lacks a driving force from within. Ones search for a life in dignity within the society that surrounds him, must be supported by positive stimulants from the community. A meaningful activity gives strength. We are proud of our African heritage.

I hope that you, who read this book, will understand why the black people in the USA hate the idea, "The American Way of life."

In the first part of this book one may tire of reading so much about my mother, Sarah. But she was one of the strongest persons I have ever met. She had only an elementary school formal education. Her travels were limited to trips to the National Baptist and Gospel Chorus Conventions over the years. Albeit her knowledge of black history from slavery to the present and her plain "mother-wit" was enormous. Her patience was endless.

I have a strong feeling that our family would have collapsed after my father's death if it had not been for the strength of Sarah Reese. I feel that I have inherited some of that toughness.

I
It Began in Church

My eyes followed my mother as she paced, phantom like, arms folded over her chest from one side of the church, back and forth, back and forth. I had never seen her dressed in black before. She was looking and acting surprisingly strange. Suddenly she stopped. With hands akimbo, she raised her tearless eyes to the ceiling. It was a gesture I had seen her make a number of times. It meant; "Now, hear me, this is how its gonna be. I'm not gonna keep repeating it. I've come to the end of my rope." She had said often that she had a direct telephone line to God and now, I thought, she was using it, for her very next words were: "God, you took him and I know you will provide. I'm gonna trust in your name because I believe you when you said, 'Lo, I'm with you in your sixth trouble and in your seventh, I will no wise leave you." And like a rehearsed chorus the congregation responded, "Amen", "That's what He said" and "Lord Jesus, help."

It was a hot sunny Sunday, the fourth day of July, 1926. My father, William Reese, was being funeralised in the Mount Vernon Baptist Church. He had fled, two years before, with his wife and eleven children from his farm in Hayneville, Alabama and had settled in one of the worst Chicago slum districts on forty-second and Federal Street. One thing that had added to mother's sorrow that day was the manner in which she had been treated by the pastor of her church.

There is one idea with which poor people are seemingly obsessed – "to be put-away nice". So, one of the first things she had father do upon reaching Chicago was to take out a Burial Insurance Policy with the Jackson Funeral Home. The cost was minimal at that time. The whole family was covered by this policy. When father entered the hospital, doctors had told my mother that there was no hope for his recovery. So, emotionally she was somewhat prepared when at six o'clock one morning two weeks later, a functionary telephoned saying that "Mr. Reese has passed." Father had taken care of the financial worries two years earlier. With a feeling of security, she telephoned the Jackson Funeral Home, within the hour, a chauffeur driven Lincoln was waiting at the curb to carry her and my brother Jackson to Cook County Hospital.

When they arrived at the entrance from which the deceased are removed, they were told by the attendant that father's remains had been carried away some twenty minutes earlier. By whom, no one could say. Mother was shocked. She remem-

bered the stories we had heard of medical students;
who had stolen or bought bodies of the dead from
Cook County Hospital. It was rumoured that some
of the hospital functionaries had been known to
sell these poor unidentified dead bodies to medical
students for observation. But this was not the case
of non-identity. Mother and Jackson returned home
with the expressed thought of calling the police.
Lula met them at the door with the news that pastor
John Johnson, shepherd of the flock of Mount
Vernon Baptist Church, had been telephoning regularly. The phone rang again before Lula had
finished her sentence. "Ah, this must be help," my
mother thought as she took the phone. Instead, she
heard a soft sugar-coated compassionate voice say;

"Hello, sister Reese, this is your pastor. Know
that God has His arms around you at this time and
He will sustain you. Now, I have lifted the burden of
arrangements from your shoulders. I have already
called MacGovock. He has your husband remains
and we will eulogise brother Reese in Mt. Vernon
on Sunday at three o'clock and – " Mother interrupted him in mid-sentence:

"Whose husband is this you talking about, yours
or mine?" There was a short pause and we heard
her say, "Well, you get on the telephone and tell
that MacGovock to release my husband's body to
the Jackson Funeral Home or I'm gonna call the
police." Pastor Johnson's sugar-coated voice now
became acidulous.

"Then you can take the funeral to some other place because I make all the arrangements for every funeral thats held in Mt. Vernon." Mother sank into a chair by the phone as she moaned:

"Father, in heaven, can it be possible?" She sat in meditation for a few minutes. Then she rang the Rev. James Madison, who had been in Chicago for a number of years. They had known Rev. Madison in Alabama, in fact when they arrived in Chicago two years earlier, they had gone to brother Madison's church. However, they did not join Monumental because, as my father said, "Madison hasn't progressed beyond the 'fire and brimstone' kind of preaching." Mother told Madison of father's passing and the trouble she was having with Johnson. And then she asked if the service could be held in Monumental and would he preach.

"Now, sister Reese," he advised, "Don't do anything in haste. Let me talk to John and I will contact you later." About a half-hour later Johnson, himself called. He apologised for his manner of treatment. He told mother that he was a little upset and that he was sorry for the worry he had caused her. He begged her forgiveness:

"Of course, you may have brother Reese's funeral here and I will be happy to preach it. Shall we say the service, as I told you, will be Sunday at three o'clock?" Mother was prepared to forgive and forget until it came to light that Rev. Johnson received fifty dollars for each dead body he was able to deliver to MacGovock's funeral home. She decided she no longer wanted to be a member of Mt. Vernon. Two weeks later she asked for a letter of dismissal. Father's passing, the treatment she had received from her pastor because he wanted to make fifty dollars, compounded to make her burden of being left with a number of small children, even heavier on that Sunday in July, 1926. Her letter of dismissal was granted. At the dinner table the day after she had received this letter, she announced.:

"We shall 'shop' around before we join another church. Of course it must be Baptist. An while we are looking for a church, we will keep our eyes open for a house in which to live". Every Sunday morning for over a month we found ourselves in a different church and congregation. Some of the churches were too formal and some of them were too 'old-fashioned' she thought. I enjoyed all of them, especially the choirs. On our fifth Sunday of wandering, we came to Pilgrim Baptist Church. One of the largest Black churches in the U.S.A.

At the door stood a tall black smiling woman who could have passed for mother's sister. "Welcome, sister," she said as she opened the door, "We hope you will enjoy our services this morning" and then when she understood that all of us lined up behind her were in the same party, she fairly chuckled as she personally led us to seats. There was a whole row empty in the centre section, three rows from the pulpit. This pew was filled by the Reese family.

I shall never forget the dramatics of that Sunday morning service.

Promptly at eleven o'clock, a tall athletic-looking type of man of sixty-five years, walked up to the pulpit. His bald patch was surrounded by curly white hair. His friendly fatherly smiling face, exuded goodness. His deep melodious clear voice, like many of the black ministers before him, inspired devotion as he intoned: "The Lord is in His Holy Temple, let all of the earth keep silent before Him." At the same time, we heard the church organ boom out the Hymn, "Holy, Holy, Holy". Glancing back, we saw a double file of white-robed men and women singing as they marched down the aisle towards the rostrum. They were lead by a tall, elegant dressed man with a white baton in his right hand. He was James A. Mundy, leader of the Pilgrim Baptist Church Senior Choir. The beginning of the service was like all the other churches we had visited. There were prayers, announcing of the weekly activities, club meetings, collection etc. Just before the Rev. S. E. J. Watson rose to give the morning sermon, the choir sang the "Hallelujah Chorus" from Handel's Messiah. I was lifted up out of my seat, I had never heard such music. When, at the end of his sermon, Rev Watson announced that the "doors of the church are now opened, who-so-ever-will, let him come", none of us were surprised to see my mother rise and go forward. The rest of us followed like sheep. We were in our second home, Pilgrim.

For 50 or 60 years after slavery, the black church was the most important institution in the life of Black people. They worked and sacrificed through many generations to erect them. Their church was free and independent. There was no white overseer to direct their every move. Most of the members lived in over-crowded slum quarters. In the streets and on their jobs, they met humiliating incidents every day of their lives. But when they entered their own church, they felt secure. In the House of God, everyone is treated with dignity.

So, it was natural that I grew up with an undying love for the church. It is with dignity that I accepted this treasure, this precious heritage that has been handed down to us by our striving and sacrificing mothers and fathers.

II
Childhood Years

My father had lived only two years after coming to Chicago. He had boarded the train at two o'clock one night in the Fall of 1923. Word had been carefully passed around that he was thinking of going to Birmingham, Alabama for the winter in order to find work. Only members of the family knew that he would not get off that train until it reached Chicago. William found a job at once in the Stockyards and began saving his money. My oldest sister Lula who would be graduating from Spelman College in Atlanta, Georgia, the June of 1924 had already planned to meet him in Chicago before she left for the Fall, Semester in 1923. As was expected, tongues began to "wag". The post mistress reported letters coming steadily from Chicago, none from Birmingham. The blow fell. It fell hard.

Two of my brothers, Jackson and Dock, were picked up by Mr. Birnett, the sheriff and placed incommunicado in the Jail in Hayneville, Alabama. Charges: "your father owes our grandfather five hundred dollars." There was no record of any loan, only his word. The words of a white man against a black man in the Alabama of 1924. The grandfather had been dead for some twenty years. He and my father had never exchanged words. Father remembered him as a sickly old man being driven around in an old buggy by his grandsons. It took every penny William had saved to get his family out of Alabama alive. The strain of trying to get lawful redress of these charges was too much. His heart had failed him.

My oldest brother, Charley, had left home in 1918. My brother, Dock, departed this life two months after my father. So Sarah was left alone with nine children. The family's financial condition was deplorable.

Mother began what later became a ritual. At the end of our dinner, we discussed the problems of the family. Lula must go to Teachers College. Sarah would find a job. Jackson would continue working in the stockyards. The rest of us would go to Keith Elementary School. "We are as poor as Job's turkey," mother said, "But we can make it with Gods help, if we stick together, all for one and one for all." It was the church that sustained and dominated our lives in those early years.

We were forced to rise at 6:30 on Sunday mornings. When we complained of being sleepy, mother said: "That's the devil sitting on your eyelids, just knock him off and get up," We awoke to the smell of hot Parker House Rolls and bacon. Sometimes we had fried salted mackerel or homemade pan sausage. Always syrup. I remember, with amusement, my mother placing rolls in the baking pan as she called each of our names, Jack, Lula, John, Henry, Rosa, Sarah, Ruth, Leon, Sue. When she had placed one roll in the pan for each of us, she began at the top again. I asked her once why she didn't just count to ten. She looked at me, smiled and said looking into space: "lie-row, catch medlow", which meant that that was her secret and she was not going to tell it to me.

We were called to the breakfast table at 7:30. Mother read a short scripture from the family Bible and said a short prayer. We attacked our hot rolls and syrup like hungry wolves. Each of us knew approximately how many rolls we could eat. To keep the peace, Sarah always had ten each for my brothers Jack, John and Henry. The rest of us were expected to consume from three to five each. But to be on the safe side, mother always had an extra pan or two in case a beggar knocked at the back door. We had plenty of bread. In addition to the Parker House Rolls, we had either a patty of home made pan sausage or a little square of fried salted mackerel or a couple slices of bacon. Invariably, we ate around our little portion of bacon, mackerel or sausage until we were nearly full and then we would take that precious morsel for the last mouthful so that we left the table with the taste of meat.

Luckily for us, when the family was searching for a church Ma had found a house only three blocks away. We could walk. Money for car fare would not be a problem. At 8:45 every Sunday morning, we were in our various Sunday school classes. At 11 o'clock, we went to the main auditorium for church services. The older ones could sit where they wished. The younger ones had to sit with my mother. We had been in Pilgrim only a short time before the ushers understood that on the left aisle, third bench from the front, the Reese clan would sit every Sunday and they reserved these seats for us. We were wide awake during the music chants and the choir's singing. When the pastor arose and announced his text, we went promptly to sleep as if on cue. Although mother said it was the devil that put us to sleep, she never disturbed us.

We were home for dinner around 2 o'clock. Then back to church for Baptist Training School at 6 o'clock. This service was followed at 8 o'clock by a musical by one of the four choirs. On our way home we received a "treat" to which we looked forward. Mother stopped at Ernies Fish Shack. Fish sandwiches were 5 cents a piece. Ma ordered ten and Mr Ernie always threw in a couple of extras. This made our day. We followed this routine for years. By then, going to church all day Sundays had become a habit we liked.

Church was our second home. We were in the church for some activity almost every day of the week except Saturdays. On Saturdays, as we grew older, we took odd jobs running errands, carrying bags of groceries, washing windows, steps, toilets and kitchens for neighbours and friends who knew our financial plight.

At 2 o'clock, with a large bag of pop-corn and peanuts, we waited in line for the Vendome Cinema or Movie, or Flicks or Pictures to open where we would see the latest edition of Rin-Tin-Tin, and Micky Mouse. To see it once was not enough. Sometimes if we were not home by 6 o'clock, Sarah would telephone Mr. Jefferson who was the ticket taker at the movie house and tell him to send her clan home. I will never forget the laughter in the movie house the first time mother did that. We were waiting for the third showing, when suddenly we heard. "All the Reese children are wanted by their mother, Sarah Reese, at 3400 Giles Avenue at once." After that Mr. Jefferson, who was an usher at Pilgrim, watched the clock for us. Saturday evenings we prepared for Sunday. We were not allowed to wash clothes, iron or sew on Sundays. "Everytime your needle goes into the cloth, you are sticking it into the wounds Jesus was given when he was crucified."

Sarah, like many other mothers, had ambitions for her children. She kept a steady look-out for suitable songs and recitations for Christmas, Easter, Thanksgiving and for other special occasions. "Be prepared if the Lord calls for your services," she would say. We understood, very soon, that Ma had a hand in "when the Lord called for our services".

But I must say that she worked hard with us. She was never too tired to listen to us perform. I remember when brother Leon was asked to recite on a children's day program. Sarah had found the "Lamplighter" by Robert L. Stevenson. She began her tutoring process at once. Our home had a long corridor that ran from the kitchen to the front room. It was all of thirty feet. Every evening, when Ma came home from work, she had Leon stand in the kitchen while she placed herself in the front room. She wanted to hear each consonant. That rehearsing paid off. On the Sunday Leon recited The Lamplighter in Pilgrim Church, his voice was as clear as Louis Armstrong's trumpet. The applause was deafening.

Although we were members of the Boy Scouts, Girl Scouts, Campfire Girls, Girl Reserves at the YWCA and handicraft classes, my chief interest was music. I had been in the children's choir for only two years when something happened that placed music above everything. I was nine years old. It was a hot Friday afternoon in August. We had been rehearsing for only a short time when the door opened and James A Mundy, the director of the Pilgrim Baptist church Senior Choir walked into my life. Mundy was one of the most colourful choral conductors in the history of Chicago music life. In the early 1930s, long before the "black is beautiful" campaign of the 1960s, Mundy was demonstrating that black is indeed beautiful. Once you have seen him, he is not easily forgotten. If you met him in the streets in the daytime, he would be immaculately donned in his accustomed stripped trousers, derby hat, kid gloves and carrying his jewelled-studded walking cane, a gift from one of England's staid music societies, on his arm. On Sunday mornings, he was usually decked out in his black swallow tails. For very special occasion, he wore his white tails.

Mundy was not only the music leader for Pilgrim. When ever white promoters wanted a "token" representation of black singers, Mundy was their contact. It was a week after his grand success in the Grant Park, where he had conducted a choir of 5000 black singers for Chicago Tribune Newspapers Grand Festival, that he honoured the children's choir with a visit. Heeding a sign from our leader, Mrs Smith, we stood up as Professor Mundy entered the room. "Children," said Mrs Smith, "Brother Mundy has something on his heart he would like to tell us about." We were as still as mice.

"Sometime this winter," stated brother Mundy, "The Senior Choir will present Mendelsohn's 'Elijah' and we need your help." A flutter of excitement spread through the group. However, with a finger to her lips, Mrs Smith brought us quickly back to attention and Mr Mundy continued. Suddenly there erupted a spontaneous outburst of laughter that Mrs Smith's finger to her lips could not stop. Mundy has announced that he needed three black angels for the "Elijah" production. Which one of us had ever heard of a black angel? I had been a regular member of a Sunday school class since I was four years old. I had never given it a thought that on all the beautiful scenes on my sunday school cards, not once had we seen a black face. All of the angels on our Biblical cards had long blond hair, blue eyes and a skin like cream. And now, here stood our great conductor saying he needed three black angels and that one of these angels must sing. When Mrs. Smith raised her hand, we stopped our laughter in order to hear what other miracles brother Mundy was asking to be rendered.

Mr Mundy became very serious. He looked sad as he asked us: "Why do you laugh? Think of all the black people God has created. Just think of all the good coloured folks who have died and gone to heaven. Surely, God has made some of them angels."

All of us knew the story of Elijah. The name of the Aria the angel would sing was, "O Rest In The Lord." Mundy advised Mrs Smith to teach the song to the entire group, just in case of a mishap. Mrs Smith wrote the words on the blackboard and we copied them down. At our next meeting she played the music. It was beautiful. Now, it was my turn to be coached by mother.

She admonished me to sing "real loud", so that I might be chosen. However, I was not too sure

that she was right this time. I had the feeling after
seeing the angels on our Sunday-school cards that
they would not sing too loud. But I did follow her
advice to learn it quickly. She borrowed a copy of
the Oratorio from one of the choir memebers so
that I could read the entire score and after dinner
Ma brought the family Bible to the table and we
heard the story of Elijah. When Mrs Smith felt that
the group knew the song well enough, she invited
brother Mundy to come to rehearsal and help
choose the singing angel.

When my turn came to "try-out", I remembered
what Ma had said about singing loud, but I forgot
it when I started. In my mind, I saw Elijah. He was
tired and hungry. Then somehow Elijah became my
old uncle, Abe, whom I loved very much. He was
90 years old. As I began to sing, "O Rest in the
Lord", I saw uncle Abe bent over his walking stick,
tired and weary and I sang to him. I was brought
out of my trance by a strong bear hug from
Professor Mundy. I had won the part of the singing
angel. I was very proud and afraid. My mother was
even more so and she intensified her coaching. So
came the big night.

The church that could seat 2500 people comfort-
ably, was packed to overflowing. There was hardly
standing room left. After the opening prayer by the
pastor, the lights were dimmed. The foot lights went
up. The spot lights flooded the stage. The orchestra
composed of Organ, Piano, Cello, Bass and two

Violins began the Overture. High up under the ceiling of the stage, unseen by the congregation, stood three small, trembling black angels. We had lights in our hands and wings on our backs. We were afraid though that we would fall down from the small niche. It seemed to have grown smaller since our rehearsal. I think I was more afraid than the other two because I had to sing. The prop men had rigged up a lift cord and each of us had a solid white silk cord fastened to the hook that was attached to our wings. I thought they would never come to our part in the Oratorio, but finally they did. We heard the introduction to the contralto Aria, "O Rest in the Lord". Almost unaware, we were in the air and gliding slowly down while I started to sing to Uncle Abe. Those hundreds of devoted black faces gazed at us, but thanks to the lights, we could not see them. We only heard and felt them. We knew that they were moved for we heard their "amens", their "hallejuhs" and their "praise God". I heard and felt their kinship.

At the end of my solo, the lights were dimmed for just a few seconds. Hurried hands loosened us from our cords, which disappeared into the ceiling. We vanished into the wings and there we stood and watched until the Oratorio was sung to the last chord.

The concert with the Black Angels, was talked about for a long time. From that time onward, there was much discussion about our religious publi-

cations carrying only white faces. When our
delegates went to the various church conventions,
they were instructed to bring up the subject. As
a result, our church literature developed colour.
Someone came up the very next Christmas with a
model for a black doll. James A. Mundy, director
of the Pilgrim's Baptist Church Senior Choir, with
his idea of black angels in Mendelsohn's "Elijah"
had much to do with that change.

III
In Unity There is Strength

As we grew older, the struggle to survive increased steadily. Sarah began to work at odd jobs, cleaning office buildings and for private families. My brother Jackson sacrificed his every personal ambition in order to support his younger brothers and sisters. Mother never could have managed without his help. Ma created what she called the "family-bank". At first, the family income was based upon the money earned by she and Jack and the pittance she received from the Family-aid Society. Lula joined them after she graduated from Chicago Teachers College. Little by little, we all began to contribute to this "Bank". Then each would receive according to his need. At least that was the theory behind the Bank idea. In practice, it was something else. The ones, who were more aggressive, benefited more. I suffered in silence, because I was too sensitive to my mother's distress and to my brother Jack's hunger for a chance to get a formal education, that was denied him because of us.

Ma demonstrated a brilliant talent in organising us. Each of us were given specific chores in the home. Mine was with the food. I have always been fascinated by food. I was constantly in the kitchen watching whoever was preparing the food. The way my mother kneaded dough enchanted me. Sometimes she gave me a bit of dough that I could bake in my little toy pan and I could use a little spice or season it as I wished. I loved to beat the eggs when she made desserts. Now and then, I was placed on a chair so that I could reach the pot and stir the greens or beans. So it was natural for my house chore to fall in the kitchen. My mother drew the face of a clock on a cardboard, "when the short hand is on 3 and the long hand on 12, light the fire under the big pot. When the short hand is a little over 4 and the long hand on 6 put in the greens. Peel the potatoes. By that time, I should be home. If I am not home by that time, turn everything off."

When I think back, the boys were very innovative. Even at the ages of nine and ten years old, they had paper routes where they sold Chicago Defender Newspapers every Friday and Saturday. John made a wagon of crate boxes. He, Henry and Leon wandered up and down the alleys of the Southside collecting discarded milk bottles, scraps, junk, old papers and sold them for pennies to the "junk-man". On Saturday mornings, they competed with other energetic hustlers of the same age for the privilege of carrying customer's groceries from the market place to their homes.

"Lady, can I help you carry your groceries, only

ten cents, please lady." They washed windows. In the alleys they found enough wood to build a step-ladder. It helped a little if they brought their own equipment. Off they would go with their home made ladder, bucket, rags and soap, "windows washed, get your windows washed-cheap!" What they earned they brought home and proudly added it to the "family bank". It was a terrible struggle and sometimes, although she hated to do it, things had to be bought on credit. And more than once bills were overdue. Occasionally bill collecters, who were usually white, would make the mistake of saying to her: "Mrs Reese, why don't you take those older children out of school and put them to work?" After she had finished telling them, why, they never brought that subject up again. The word passed from one old collector to the new: "don't mention her taking the children out of school and put them to work."

I remember during this time, we had a number of white charity or case workers as they are called. Sarah was receiving a small pittance for each child who was still in school. These case workers had a habit of coming unannounced early in the morning or rather late at night. At times there would be no grown-ups at home. So, mother had installed a "I don't know, you must ask my mother," code. Some of these workers, to their regret, had suggested to mother that she should get married again.

"Mrs Reese, you are still young and a fine looking

woman, why don't you get some man to help you
with all of these children, it must be very hard for
you." Ma concluded, and rightly so, that this was
the cause of the early and late visits. They were
trying to find out if she had a man coming to the
house and if so, she would lose the little pittance
she was getting from the social agency. I shall never
forget one of those early visits.

It was six o'clock. The house was bustling with
preparations for school and work. Ma was in the
kitchen getting breakfast ready. And from the
kitchen she was trying to direct our activities "Leon,
change those dirty socks; John, put on a clean shirt;
Ruth, make your bed;" etc, when the door bell rang.
"Somebody answer the door," she yelled. When the
door was opened, in walked our caseworker with
eyes dotting from one direction to the other as she
continued to walk through the house. "Ma, its the
welfare woman," Rosa called. Ma stopped stirring
the grits and went to meet this woman. Just as the
poor woman turned from peeking into one of the
bedrooms, she and Sarah stood face to face. I had
seldom seen Ma so angry.

"What do you want in there?", mother asked, as
she advanced on this woman, her hands akimbo.
Leopard-like, mother crept forward muttering
through clenched teeth as the woman nearly frightened out of her wits, slowly backed up.

"I know exactly what you are looking for. You
are trying to see if I have a man in here. I have

told you all there is no man in this house. I am a Christian woman and this is a Christian home and now you little white heifer, if you ever come to this house again at this hour in the morning, when I'm trying to get these children off to school and myself off to work, I'm gonna whip your ass until you shit, you hear me?" By that time, the poor creature had backed out of the front door, which John was holding open for her. The next day the welfare office called and said: "Mrs Reese, we have some papers that you must sign, what is the best time for our worker to call on you?"

The next day at 5 p.m. a well-dressed black woman smiled at my mother as she shyly looked around.

Although she would be very tired at the end of her working day, she always took the time to question us on happenings at school. What did the teacher stress to day in history? Did she say anything about Frederick Douglas, Nat Turner or Harriet Tubman. If our teacher had omitted certain facts, and this happened often with white teachers, she would fill us in. Carter G. Woodson's "The Negro in our History" was our second Bible. Sarah tried very hard to prepare us for the problems we would meet in the American community. She encouraged us to talk about the difficulties we met during the day, whether they were with white or black people. If one of us had a question, it became the problem of the entire family. We discussed it at the dinner table. We were keenly aware of the injustices meted out to black people. Hardly a day passed without one of us having an incident to report. It's sad to think of how much time black people must spend, if they will survive, thinking about their existence in a world governed by whites.

Two weeks before my graduation from Keith Elementary School, I found myself in real trouble. Mrs MacManerny, our history teacher, in order to keep the class occupied while she gossiped with a colleague, asked the class to write a theme on the subject: "What does the American Flag Mean to You?" And she had announced that "when you have finished your theme, place it on my desk and go quietly out of the room. Make as little noise as possible in the corridors as you leave the building." I thought to myself – this should be very easy and I came to the point in my first sentence: "The American flag means absolutely nothing to black people. To me its just some stripes of cloth, red and white, sewn together. There are some stars in the corner." I signed my name and left the room as quietly as possible.

Upon entering the school the next morning, the teacher on hall duty directed me to go to my history teacher. As I entered the room, I knew something was wrong. Mrs MacManerny, looking over her glasses, waved a sheet of white paper at me and said, "What is the meaning of this?" I moved a little closer so that I could see. It was my theme. "What is the meaning of this" she repeated.

Meekly, I answered, "You told us to write what the American flag means to us."

"And this is what the flag of the United States of America means to you?"

"Teacher", I murmured, "That flag is for the white people, it does not help black people." She stood there with her mouth open for a while and then she said:

"We will see about that, you come with me." And off we marched to the principal's office. She handed Mr. Langley the paper. We both stood silent while he read it. When he had finished, he turned to me and said.

"Ruth, you must go home until one of your parents can come in and talk to me." I knew there was no one at home, so I walked to our church. On the way, I thought. Why all the fuss? Wasn't I supposed to write what I was thinking? Did she expect me to lie? I have never been able to figure out why any black person should be expected to feel a deep patriotism for a land that has taken everything from him including his name. When I left the church to go home, I felt badly because I knew I was adding another burden to my mother's shoulders. When she came home from work, I told her what had happened to me. She turned to me shook her head, sighed deeply and then smiled at me. I will never forget the feeling of relief that flooded over me when I saw that smile. And then she said:

"Lord, child, you hit the nail on the head, but you must learn that there are sometimes when it is better not to let people know exactly what you are thinking, especially, if they have the upper hand." That is something we learned from our slave ancestors, sometimes its better to bow your head than to be tied to a stake and be beaten to death." The meaning of the American Flag was the central discussion at dinner that day.

My mother followed me to school the next day. After she had talked with Mr Langley, the principal, I was allowed to come back to school, but I would be barred from taking part in the festivities. He would not present me my diploma, but I would receive it in the mail. My credits would be sent to Phillips High School where I would enter in September, if I wished.

There was one good thing about the whole episode. I missed the class parties, but I was able to find a job for the summer before the market was flooded with other students. For that reason, my financial condition would be better in September.

IV
Poor But Proud

When I entered Phillips High School in September, I was much relieved to find that there was no evidence of the scandal I had made in Keith, about that American Flag. As I had left home that morning, Ma had advised me to "get as many black teachers as possible. In the first place, they will be more demanding and in the second place, they will show a greater interest in you personally, because they have had to struggle so much harder than the white teachers to get into the same position, they probably know their subjects better." It was common knowledge that poor white teachers were shunted off into black schools and that good white teachers in black schools, most of them, were simply waiting to be assigned into their own districts.

New students were instructed to assemble in the gymnasium of the school. Here we were given instruction about registering for classes. On a large chart on the wall, one could read how many credits per semester one must have in order to graduate within four years. In addition, the chart showed: What subjects, how many hours, how many credits, time of day, room and teacher. Also students were allowed to choose their own subjects. I had signed up for the Liberal Arts Course, but I elected to take typing for an elected subject.

I knew the reputation of some of the teachers. For my English I chose Robertann B. Cuthbert, one of the best English teachers that has been in Chicago. For years, High Park High School, where blacks were not wanted, had been trying to woo her, but she chose to serve her own people. To her and my sister Lula, I owe my love of books. I became an avid reader. Ben Mosby, I chose for Civics. For me, Mosby placed the mechanics of social structure and its relation to blacks in perspective. For science and mathematics I enrolled with Mr Pierce. I had two music teachers, Mildred Bryant Jones and Aline Burch. And of course I had physical education. I took typing for an elected subject because I thought it would enhance my chances for a better job after school. Up to that time I had done house cleaning. After a year I was a fairly good typist.

It was my second week. I opened the "help wanted" section of the daily paper and read: "wanted, coloured girl, light house work after school." I applied the same day and was hired.

"How old are you?" the woman asked me.

"Sixteen", I replied without blinking an eye. Even at age eleven I had been passing for sixteen in order to get a job. I was hired and was told to come the next day. I can't even remember her name anymore. She took me over the five-room apartment explaining what she wanted me to do. However, I noticed that she followed me after that watching my every move. By that time in my life, I knew how to clean a house and I was a little annoyed at her standing over me the whole time. I honestly did not mean to be impudent, I just wanted her to know that she could trust me. And so I said to her:

"Please, there is no need to stand over me while I work. Just tell me what you wish done, and I'll do it. You don't have to watch me."

"Get your things and get out of here." she hissed. 'You owe me for an hour and a half. That's seventy-five cents." There was a short intake of breath as she stood with her mouth agape. She was staring at me as if she had not heard. Then she became aware of the meaning of my out-stretched hand. She turned suddenly, strided into her bedroom. She returned within a few minutes and flung a one dollar bill on the small table that stood near me. Luckily, I had a quarter. I picked up the dollar bill and laid my quarter in its place. She stood silently as I left, but I could feel her eyes boring in my back. That was the end of my first job as a cleaning girl in a white family. I was four-teen years old. I had wanted to venture out.

I had been working at odd jobs in homes of coloured professionals since I was ten and eleven years old. Every Saturday from ten o'clock to two o'clock I cleaned up their dirt. No matter how pleased they seemed, I was given thirty-five cents per hour and sometimes some of their "cast-offs". At least I had earned enough to give the family bank one dollar and still had enough to pay for an afternoon at the Mickey Mouse Movie House and a gallon bag of popcorn and peanuts.

From school friends, I heard that working conditions in white families were sometimes better, especially if the family was "well-off" economically. The house-help was given specific tasks. In black families, the lady of the house usually worked along with me, however I was always called to perform the nasty jobs. One minute I would find myself working with the garbage in the kitchen and suddenly I would be ordered to wash the toilet. Or, I would be handed a tooth brush and instructed to scrape the trash from the corners of the living room.

After the experience I had with my first venture working for a white family, my mother felt I needed some basic instructions. "Be pleasant, but never friendly," she said to me. "Never start a conversation with them unless it's to ask about something concerning your job. Find out the first day what your job is. Don't do any laundry and don't wash any windows. I won't have you hanging out of windows, its too dangerous for a child. Always do your job as well as you can. You may think the pay is too little, however, if you accept, you must be fair and do your task as best you can. If its all too hard

just quit and come home." With these instructions,
I went to my second stint in a white family.

It lasted all of two weeks. When Mrs Walcott
had hired me, she had said that I could be free
on Sundays and Mondays. Everything was going
beautifully. She liked my work. I was happy. Then
on Saturday night of the second week, when I was
just getting ready to go to bed, the telephone rang;
Mrs Walcott's voice:

"Ruth, come to me on Monday. Some friends of
mine are coming for dinner. You may take Tuesday
off." I had left her home about five hours earlier.

"I'm sorry, Mrs Walcott, but my choir is having
a concert on Monday, I won't be able to come."

"Then you don't need to come to me anymore.
I'll find a girl who can come when I want her."

"Thanks very much." I replied and I held the
phone waiting, because I had been taught that it
was courteous to wait for the caller to say goodbye
and hang up first. I waited for her goodbye but it
never came. She simply hung up. Naturally, I began
to reflect. I had never lost a job because of my work.
In fact all of the persons for whom I had worked,
praised my work very highly. But here I was, after
only two weeks out of a job again. I began to understand a little about the psychology of the mind of
these white bosses I was meeting close up for the
first time. The blacks for whom I had worked, had
shown an entirely different attitude towards me. To
the white bosses, I was not subservient enough for

their liking. I was not acting like a slave. I must be kept in my place. And I must be conscious of that place at all times.

Finally, I found what I thought at first was a perfect situation. I had never asked any of my school friends to help me in finding a job. My very best friend, Aramantha Chaney, had been working for the same family for more than three years. One day I found enough courage to ask Aramantha to help me find a job. A few days later, she informed me that the sister of her boss would like me to come and work for her. I duly reported the next day to Mrs. Etterhagen. Everything went swimmingly for a time. She tried to hold me in conversation a little too much for my liking, but I attributed that to the fact that they had known Aramantha so long. I tried to be civil, although I was annoyed. My mood is not too good when I'm cleaning even in my own house. I was on guard the whole time because I did not wish to disappoint Aramantha. But sometimes Mrs Etterhagen could be irksome. One day in all seriousness she asked me:

"Ruth, why do you struggle so hard?" I looked at her without responding for a while and then she continued: "You do beautiful work. I could give you two or three days work each week and I am sure I have friends who would hire you. You could work full time." I would not trust myself to look at her, for I was trying desperately to hide my disgust when I said:

"Really, I would not wish to spend the rest of my life cleaning floors – " I was happy that the telephone rang at that moment. That conversation stopped there. Then on the very next day, she interrupted my work.

"Ruth, come, you must see this. I think its so cute." She placed her forefinger to her lips as we tipped-toed to her daughter's room. She gently pushed the door ajar. Debra, her eight year old daughter sat on the floor surrounded by a dozen or so dolls. These dolls were of all nationalities and sizes. One of them stood out from the rest. This one was as black as night with "black-sambo" features. Debra sat like a queen entertaining guest at a tea party. She was chattering away, changing the inflections in her voice as the conversation passed from one doll to the next. It really was a cute scene. And I wondered afterwards why the mother would spoil it. I had noted without her remarking it, that the black doll was doing the serving. But just in case I had missed the point, Mrs Etterhagen whispered to me:

"Debra calls the serving girl, Aramantha."

"Your daughter," I replied unsmiling, "Will someday become a writer, she had a very strong imagination." She did not comment. I went back to my work. When I had finished my chores for the day, she said as she handed me my pay:

"Here is your money, you need not come to work for me anymore."

"Thanks very much", was all I managed to say as I rushed to get away. I felt tears mounting up and I would rather have died than for her to see me cry. Sitting on the street corner on my way home I wondered what in the hell else did she want from me. She had told me herself that my work was beautiful. When I thought a little about it, she should have been paying me much more. I was a fifteen year old cleaning as a full grown woman. She would have had to pay an adult double what she was paying me. I had not asked her the reason she was firing me, but I wanted to know the truth.

So, without telling my friend, Aramantha, anything of the doll incident, I begged her to find out from her employer why her sister had let me go. A few days later; Aramantha came with the answer. She said her employer had called Mrs Etterhagen and the lady had said,

"Ruth is a very good worker. I liked her work, but she is too poor to be so proud. I just could not stand it."

Well, the lady hired me to do a job. I did it well, she said. I was very happy with myself.

V
Years in Between

Before October, 1935, I had not seriously thought of music as a career. Music was fun. It weas recreation. It was easy. It was a natural thing to do. I had been a member of the Children's Choir, of the Junior Choir and now I was a member of the Young Peoples Choir. "Gold and silver have I none, but such as I have, give I Thee", had been my motto. At least that had been mother's motto for us. We were a poor family. We did not have money to place in a collection plate, but we had time and talent. Serve! So the Reese family became known as a "good church-working family" in the Chicago Baptist church circles. Our church bustled with activity and the Reese's were a part of the action.

One of the traditions of the Pilgrim Church was the annual Religious Revival Meeting held the first two weeks in October. "The Church of Tomorrow" would be the theme of the meeting. All of the choirs would participate at some point during the fifteen days. However, because of the theme, "The Church of Tomorrow", and the Young Peoples Choir was asked to replace the Senior Choir for the opening

Sunday morning service. In our rehearsal the previous week, the conductor had chosen two anthems – "Lift Up Your Head, Oh Ye Gates" and "The Lord is My Light." For the Invitational Hymn, we would sing, "Have Thine Own Way, Lord". To our utter surprise, the pastor of the church had changed his announced text and was now fervently preaching the Prodigal Son story. As the pastor neared the end of his talk, the conductor whispered to me:

"Ruth, can you think of a song that you could sing that would be more appropriate than 'Have Thine Own Way?' "

"Lord, I'm Coming Home?"

"Yes," he said, "You sing that alone, the choir will hum the chorus." As was the custom, the pastor ended his sermon by saying, "the door of the church is now open-who-so-ever will, let him come now and unite with us." The deacons, all twenty four of them, rose from the first row of their seats and faced the congregation. The pastor walked down and stood in front of the deacons waiting to welcome new comers. The organ began to play. I started and sang:

"I've wandered far away from God, now I'm coming home." Forty-six people joined Pilgrim church that Sunday morning. It was somewhat of a sensation. Never before or after, have so many united with the church at one time. At the moment, I thought nothing of it. I had not thought of it as

something special, on my part. But, after the service
when I went to the robe-room to change into street
clothes, Edward Boatner, the Senior Choir
conductor was waiting for me.

"Ruth," he said, "That was a wonderful thing
you did this morning. You have something special.
You have a God-given talent and you must use it.
And you must train it. You don't wish to devote
your time to that sort of singing. Your voice is too
good for that."

I did not bother to ask him what was wrong with
that type of singing. I knew what he meant. He was
seeing me as potential material for his Senior Choir.
The repertoire of the Senior Choir under Edward
H. Boatner, who had taken over after James A.
Mundy left, was the same. It consisted of mainly
Oratorios of Bach, Handel and Mendelsohn and
classic anthems and the most highly stylised *Negro*
Spirituals.

"One must study the classics if one is to have a
musical career," he was saying, "When can you
come to me for music lessons?" And without waiting
for my reply, he continued: "Come to me on Wednesday, after school, say three o'clock."

"That is impossible, I must work after school."

"Call, and find out if you can come two or three
hours later." "But I must wait a little." Sensing my
trouble he said:

"Don't worry about the money, you can pay me
when you get it." I knew that was impractical. I

hated buying anything on credit, but I gave in. The "music bug" had indeed bitten me. So I said:

"I'll be there."

Boatner did not allow me to sing for the first six months. We spent our lesson time doing exercises that would build and strengthen muscles singers use most. He was a devotee of the Yawn-Stretch Method. After years of experience, I can say that Boatner was one of the finest "voice builders" one could hope to meet. To my sorrow, after only one year and a half, he left Chicago to go to New York and greener pastures. There was one important thing he had done for me – he aroused within me a genuine interest in music. I wanted to sing. I wanted a singing career. I wanted to sing various forms. Classic, Spirituals, Gospel, Blues, and Jazz. Why not? Immediately after Boatner left Chicago, I began my search for a new voice teacher.

A friend recommended a Mrs. Sainger, who had had a number of sucessful students. I called her for an audition, and was accepted as a pupil. In fact she seemed somewhat excited about my possibilities. At the end of my second session with her, she asked me to sit for a minute, she had something very important to talk to me about my singing career.

"Ruth," she began, "If I had your voice, I would let nothing stop me. Now listen, I have a friend. He knows absolutely nothing about music, he just likes to be around artists. His name is Sam. You would not be bothered with him more than once a month.

If I talk to him, I am sure that he would pay for your lessons and give you enough money on which to live so that you won't have to work after school. In that way you would have all your time for study. Think about it and tell me at your next lesson. Or call me and I will have Sam come and hear you." And then she spent a considerable amount of time telling me stories of very famous artists, many of whom I knew, who had made it by the help of some rich man who was interested in being around artists.

Now, I do agree with you that at my age, I should have known about the facts of life. I know its sounds naive. But I did not have the faintest idea of what Mrs. Sainger was implying. I rushed home to tell my mother about my first offer of a scholarship to study music. In my exuberance, I did not notice the change that gradually came over her. Vaguely, I saw her fold her arms over her breast. Her lips closed in a sort of pucker. And suddenly, I noticed her breathing became more pronounced as if she had been running. Finally, I finished. I was waiting for her to say, "thank God" or something of that sort. Instead, she said not a single word to me. She went straight to the telephone. I was flabbergasted when I heard the tone of her voice as she asked:

"Is this Mrs. Sainger, the voice teacher?" There was a short pause. Then I heard her continue: "This is the mother of Ruth Reese. She has just told me about the proposition you have offered her for a musical career. Now, I don't know what kind of woman you are, and I don't care, but I want you to know that no daughter of mine is going to whore for singing lessons, you hear me?" With that she banged the telephone on to the cradle. I was never so embarrassed in my life. I hoped that I would never see or hear from Mrs. Sainger again. I was thoroughly ashamed.

In the meantime, my financial burden had become lighter. True to her word, Mrs Foley engaged me to work in her home on Mondays, Fridays and Saturdays assisting her regular house maid. Meanwhile, Mrs. Bousfield had arranged for me to receive sixteen dollars each month from the "Aid to Fatherless Children Fund" as long as I remained in school and made good grades. Needless to say the sixteen dollars went into the "Family Bank." At last I was able to follow Boatner's advice and began to study the piano. "Don't be a dumb singer who cannot find her own notes on the piano," he had said to me.

Being a little more secure financially, I literally plunged into school and church-sponsored activities. I was a girl reserve, a camp fire girl, a girl scout. I engaged in sports.

In my third year in High School, I was elected secretary of the student council, which was composed of all officers of the various student clubs. Looking back now, I understand how clever our principal was and how he manipulated us. At the beginning of each semester, he called the officers of the Council to his private office, where we were served snacks and lemonade. In a most solicitous manner, he outlined his program for the entire school body and he led us to believe that he could accomplish these aims only with the help of the student council. When we, as officers, carried these ideas back to the Student Council, not as "what the Principal said", but what we as officers thought, the Council members accepted them and pledged to carry them out to the letter.

Two important things happened to me during my senior year in Phillips. The first, I was directed by the leader of the Senior Choir of Pilgrim Church, to study the three altosarias in Handel's Messiah for the Christmas Concert. If I made a good showing, I would surely be elevated from the Young Peoples Choir to the Church's Senoir Choir. The second great event was when I was elected president of my graduation class. It was the first time in the history of Phillips that a girl had been given that honour.

On graduation night in the school auditoriaum before parents and friends of three hundred and twenty-five seniors, I gave my first rousing public speech. For a number of months, I carried the comments on my speech made by the Chicago Defender Newspaper in my purse and would pull it out and show it at the least provocation. Also on the night of my graduation, I received a Ribbon. I had never been late or absent during my four years. My finishing at Keith Elementary school had been a thud, my graduation from Phillips High School had truly been a Bang. I was naive enough to think then that life would be rosy.

VI
Sarah Ventures into Politics

Ma had never talked to us so much about Hayneville in Alabama as she did that day. We knew it
was a feeling of relief that had brought on this
flood of conversation. Jackson had just come in with
Leon, who had spent the night along with 7 of his
playmates, in the community jail. They had played
basketball at the Wabash Y.M.C.A. They had won.
One the way home they were still discussing their
victory and arguing about who had the most shots
and who had made the best plays.

Then suddenly, they found themselves betting
on, of all things, who could piss the longest, and
they decided to prove it. They lined up, seven
abreast, one block from home. They were having
so much fun, they failed to hear or see a police car,
with lights out containing two robust Irish Cops,
who crept up behind them. All seven were carted
off to jail. Luckily, they were all released into the
custody of a relative the next morning.

Our family discussion that day was the need for
blacks on the police force. An understanding police
would have talked to the boys or else escorted them

home instead of off to jail. Even though we were
frightened when a neighbour called and said he had
seen Leon taken into the "paddy-wagon" around
11 o'clock, we were much relieved to hear that it
was because of some trivia instead of the more
serious crimes being committed by boys 13 and 14
years of age in Chicago at that time.

Suddenly, Ma was discussing her life in Alabama.
Sensing her mood, we brought forth questions we
had held back for a long time. We heard about
Hayneville, the little village where she was born.
Less than five thousand people lived there. Eighty
per cent of them were black, but the other twenty
per cent had total power. We heard the gruesome
history of the South, the Grandfather Clause that
kept blacks from voting, the Poll Tax, the terror of
the Klu Klux Klan. Ma talked about the Democrats
and Republicans and politicians, who she placed at
the bottom ring of the human ladder. She told us
about the little one-room school house that had to
be rebuilt every two or three years because whites
set fire to it in the middle of the night. And then in
1918 the Boll Weevil epidemic destroyed every crop.
"We decided then to pull up stakes. We were determined that our children would have a chance to
make something of themselves."

"We always read the Chicago Defender News-
paper even then. That paper was outlawed in
Hayneville. Anyone caught selling it could be jailed.
But you know, God will provide. Every train

running North to South and back, had black porters and waiters. These black brothers wrapped copies of the Defender in oil paper and placed them in the bottom of the garbage containers. They knew only blacks would be handling the refuse bags. Then every Tuesday God sent, without fail, we watched for old Leroy Bailey."

"That poor old soul's back was bent from years of picking up trash in the 'white only' park. On Tuesdays, he was one of those who were assigned by the Sanitation Department to dispose of the garbage from the Chicago Four O'Clock Special. When we saw old Leroy coming with his lips puckered and singing his favourite tune, 'A Charge to Keep I have, A God To Glorify', we knew that the 'World's Greatest Weekly' was safely hidden in the inner pocket of his over-alls. There were many stories about what had been transported in those pockets Effie, his wife, had made. But on Tuesdays, this pocket held retrieved copies of the smuggled black newspaper 'The Chicago Defender.' "

"Lord, child, you cannot imagine how we waited for that paper. You will never know how we felt when we read it. We, your father and I, sat in the kitchen after you children had been put to bed. We read it from cover to cover, even the adds. And then the next day we passed it on to 'safe neighbours'. Every week Mr. Robert Abbott, the editor of the paper, extolled blacks to come North. Come to Chicago, the promised land. And so we came. But

we soon learned that we had exchanged a concerned
slum for an indifferent one. Your father died of
heart attack only two years after coming here. He
grieved himself to death over the way they cheated
him out of his land. You see what we have had to
do in order to survive here."

"You children have not been able to go to the
playground after school like other children your age.
You have to go to jobs. But you are not paid properly. I work every day. I'm not paid fairly either.
We are all exploited to the hilt. But we manage.
Our heads are above the water. We are as poor as
'Job's Turkey', but that's not our fault. We work
hard everyday. We worked hard in Alabama also.
This family has always been hard workers. In
Alabama, we worked our farm, but could never get
ample pay for our produce. The buyers were all
white. We were forced to accept whatever deal they
made. They were all united on what price would
be offered to us. Here, in Chicago, each of you have
some kind of job after school. However, in every
instance, the pay is inadequate. Why? There is a
cause for everything. And I have concluded that in
our case, it is the system under which we live.

"You hear them talk much about something
called 'The American Way of Life'. There is something definitely wrong, under this 'American Way
of Life' for black people. We can't do anything to
change it, but we don't have to accept it. We can

challenge it and try with the help of God to beat it."

"What's this 'System' you keep talking about?" I asked puzzled.

"That is just the trouble. You can't say exactly what or who it is. The enemy is there. You know he's there. He's invisible. In spite of everything though, there has never been a day when my pot was not full of something to eat. And you children have had sufficient clothes to keep going. And for that, I am thankful to God."

For a moment we forgot our troubles and smiled to each other. We had heard mother make this declaration so many times. And it was true. Our family was never hopelessly hungry, but we did wish sometimes for some of the delicacies of which we saw and read about daily. But, what could we say. All of us knew that Sarah was dissatisfied with our lot. We also knew that she was determined that her children would never see any sign of weakness in her. So, we ate what was in the pot and said, "Gracious Lord, we thank Thee for the food we are about to receive for the nourishment of our body, amen."

When Ma was in a specially good humour, we enjoyed teasing her about our supply. Once when she enjoined us to be "thankful for what you have", Susie, who seldom said anything at the family gatherings, provoked laughter, even from Sarah, when she, straight-faced, commented, "Come to think of it, I could be much more thankful if I had a little more for which to be grateful."

"You must thank God for your health and strength", Ma stated gravely.

We waited. Any one of us could have given mother's next speech. We had heard it so many times and we never ceased to wonder just how she came to settle on such a theory. According to Sarah, the rich had more afflictions than any other group of people on earth. There was not a single normal individual among them. They all have ulcered stomachs, none were really happy. And she was positive that most of them would exchange a great deal of their wealth for the kind of health her children enjoyed. John was waiting for her to finish and then he said:

"I'll gladly give brother Rockefeller my porridge this morning in exchange for his ulcers and all the rest of his possessions."

"You were always a fool," Ma answered. We laughed. We ate our porridge. We felt good. We were happy. It was good to have the fellowship of each other. Sarah was absolutely right when she said our pot was always full of something, collard greens, turnip greens, rutabagas, cabbage cooked with pig feet and hog knuckles. And then, one day, we had a stroke of luck which lasted for nearly two years. John came home with the news that he had found a new after school job.

"Hallelujah", cried Jack. John had been

borrowing from him for weeks. "What kind of a job?"

"Picking chickens after school and on Saturdays."

"How much will they pay you?"

"I'll get fifty cents and two chickens a day and three on Saturdays."

"Be sure you get fat ones, brother and stick one in your bosom when you get the chance," advised Leon.

"That's the devil talking", injected Lula. "But won't we get tired of chicken eating it every day?"

"Now, who ever heard of niggers getting tired of eating fried chicken?" mused Rosa as if she was talking to herself.

"When do you start?" asked Henry.

"Next Saturday."

"The Lord brings Sunday", laughed Henry.

"Don't play with the Lord's name", cautioned Ma, however, all of us could see that she was as pleased as the rest of us. We looked forward to our Sunday dinners. We prayed that John would hold that job for a long time. Only once in a while our dinner would be spoiled by hungry guests. Sarah, sensing sometimes the plight of some of her church members, would invite them for Sunday dinner. She had cured us but she had not cured herself, of bringing unexpected guests home at mealtime. She never said to us, "Don't bring your friends home at meal time," our friends were welcomed at all times. Howbeit, she made a simple rule – whoever had invited a friend must divide his portion of the dessert with his invited guest. No one of us minded how much of the greens were eaten by visitors. But to divide our portion of the Sweet Potato Pie or the Lemon Cream Pie was a horse of another colour. We had learned to say to friends who would follow us home at mealtime, "see you later, alligator."

Then there was the time our family pot did run over. It was election time. Leon laughingly described it to a friend later.

"You know, man, we discovered that the porterhouse is a beef steak. It's not a hotel. We found out the T-bone and the porterhouse comes from the cow. And do you know there is a part of lamb called, 'saddle'? And I know what you guys thought the 'loin' refers to. Man, the loin is a beef-roast that sure taste good baked in its own gravy. And man, just think we have been 'gnawing' on neck bones all these years pretending its chicken."

Yes, election time was a good time for the family for one reason only; we had something that could be exploited. We lived in an old house with a large basement. It had been serving the family for years as a dumping station. It was cluttered from front to back. Then one Sunday morning someone told Sarah about an old woman who had been placed in the street because she was unable to pay her rent. Sarah sent the boys home from church with orders to clean the basement. When John reminded her that it was Sunday, she quoted from St. Mark:

"Is it lawful to do good on the Sabbath day or to do evil? The Sabbath was made for man and not man for the Sabbath."

And so, they shrugged their shoulders and went home to clean the basement. Sarah went in search of sister Fisher. When she arrived on the spot, neighbours had taken her in for the night.

"Good," said Sarah, "That will give me a little time to get ready for the poor old soul."

On their way home, the boys collected some of their buddies to help them clean the basement. The ground floor of our house was surprisingly spacious. There was one large enclosed room at the front. The rest was a space of about thirty feet long and twelve to fifteen feet wide. The cleaning brigade washed the ceiling, walls and floor. The next morning, they bought an inexpensive quick-drying powdered-blue paint. Sarah smiled her approval, when she saw the results. When the boys surveyed the finished job, Leon exclaimed,

"Now, why didn't we think of this a long time ago. Man, we could play some mean pool in here."

"It's too late now," Jackson said, "The Good Samaritan has taken over."

Two days later sister Fisher moved in and what a lesson she taught Sarah in a very short time. Luckily for Ma, she had promised the room to sister Fisher only "until you are able to find a place to live". Ma had thought it unchristian to lock the kitchen door that led to the basement. "If there is a fire, the old soul might be trapped," she reasoned. Within the week, small things began to disappear from mother's room. Every morning, around five-thirty, the most pungent odour of incense floated through the house. But the weirdest of all, were her voodoo-like meetings. When she had these meetings, she placed all sorts of bone relics outside of her door. It took a little time, but we finally got her out of the house. Again, the boys were ordered to scrub the basement from top to bottom.

"What if that old lady has put some 'jinks' on this basement," joked Leon.

"Just use good, soapy hot suds," Sarah replied. "Put a little lye in the water. That will get rid of all the evil spirits. The Lord is my Shepherd." When we saw Leon's jaws the next morning we were uneasy, to say the least. He had the mumps. Ma told him: "Everyone has the mumps sooner or later. It was time for you to have them. Its natural."

For a time, we had the most popular house in the block. The politicians came, first the Republicans and then the Democrats. A Presidential Election would be held in November. It is a known fact that the whole country stands on its head during the election campaign. It is a regular circus. The whole Country gets involved. Orthodox and unorthodox methods are used. Scandals are uncovered and exposed on both sides. The amount of money

used is astronomical. Real issues are never
discussed. So it was that fall in Chicago. The news
of our clean, roomy basement spread.

When the republican precinct captain
approached Sarah about meeting in our ground-
floor, she, as was usual, called a family meeting.
She appreciated the fact that the precinct captain
and many of the ward workers were black, but she
knew that they had no power. They received their
orders from the big boss down town and those
masters were all white. They were the overseers of
the "system" she hated.

"All right", declared Sarah, "They wish to use
us. How can we use them? What can we get out of
it? It's 'tit' for 'tat'. They will 'tit' us and we shall
try to 'tat' them more than they 'tit' us." When
Mr. Jones came for his answer about the use of the
basement, Ma bade him welcome, took him down
and showed him the basement. He agreed with her
that the place needed better lighting both in the
entrance and in the room. There were no chairs
and there must be coal for that fat-bellied furnace.
Mr. Jones promised that all would be arranged.
And it was done. The electricians came. The coal
bin was filled to overflowing with "grade-A" coal.

If anyone had asked Sarah where she stood politically, she would have answered, republican, not
that she had any great love for them. She would be
the first to admit that no greater hypocrites walked
on earth than republicans. In Alabama, her home,

Democrats had complete control. She hated the very word. They had invoked the "Grandfather Clause" – any black can vote if his great grandfather had voted in any election. My mother, as most blacks in America, had no knowledge of the name of her great grandfather, whose name was taken from him when he was put on the auction block upon landing in the United States. He was forced to accept the name of his owner. All she was able to pass on to us was the name, "Gold Coast", which is now Ghana. No, Sarah voted because she felt strongly that it was her duty and right to vote. The Republican Party was the lesser evil of the two.

In fact, Sarah had a theory. The ones with the power in both parties were white and when they got together blacks were black. It made little difference to the man of colour which party came to power. But there was one thing upon which you could count. If there was a black man or woman on either ballot, he or she would get Sarah's vote. She would religiously bring her sample ballot home and Jack would go through it and show her how to "split" her ticket. Once she voted for a Black man who was running for president of the United States on an Independent Ballot. When she told Mrs Coleman, her neighbour that she had voted for brother Jefferson J. Johnson for President of the United States, sister Coleman laughed, shook her head and said, "sister, you have just thrown away your vote."

"Well," replied Sarah acidly, "If he has the nerve to run for president, I have the guts to give him my vote." And because sister Coleman had not bothered to go to the polls at all, Sarah added tartly, "at least, I did my duty today. I went to the polls and cast my ballot for someone." Finally, the day came for the first meeting of the Republicans. The place was cosy, warm, well-lighted, with comfortable chairs. They had started at 8 o'clock. By 10, they were out. When Jack came down to lock up, he was surprised to find a collection with a note saying, "for cleaning up." "Thats us incorporated", yelled Leon and without a single complaint, they set to work to make the basement "spick" and "span" for the next meeting. The next day, lo and behold, the democratic precinct captain knocked at the door.

When Ma opened the door there stood little Mr. Ellis. I felt a great pity for him as he stood there, hat in hand, asking to use a part of our house for a meeting of democrats. I just knew Ma would say some hard thing to him and send him packing. On the contrary, Mr Ellis received a civil answer. Yes, Mr Ellis was black. Closing the door Sarah said laughing, "there now, it looks like we are in the political business, will the meeting come to order."

"What you are thinking of doing is absolutely impossible," warned Lula.

"Nothing is impossible," we all chirped as if we had rehearsed the cue. Mother laughed as she heard

her own words. "Nothing is impossible," hurled
back at her. "I know we must find out from brother
Jones which days he will want the place. After all,
it was he who fixed the place up with lights and all
of the rest. So, if we can get a little "do-re-me" from
both sides, so much the better for us. Its only two
months before the election. We had better start
cracking.

"Suppose the Republicans don't like the idea of
the Democrats meeting here?," interposed Lula.

"Thats my business. Its my basement."

"But surely, they will find out."

"You never can tell. Maybe, Mr. Jones sent Mr.
Ellis. You are dealing with politicians now. We shall
say nothing and just wait and see 'which way the
crow flies'."

The Republicans were installed for Tuesdays and
Fridays and the Democrats were given Wednesdays
and Saturdays. Of course the Republicans were the
richer of the two parties. However, from both, the
family received coupons. Coupons for food, coupons
for clothes, for shoes, for furniture, for bed linen,
for coal, for cinema. There were seemingly coupons
for everything. The coal bin was running over, but
neither party ever found that out, for when the coal
bin started to be filled, the excess coal was carried
up to the attic. Each party left a donation for the
cleaning up in addition to the fee for the use of the
place. Then John got a bright idea. He took Mr.
Jones off to the side and asked him if he thought

his members might like to sip lemonade during their meeting. John put the same question of Mr. Ellis. They both accepted the idea.

With enthusiasm my sisters Rosa, Susie, Sarah and I with Ma as supervisor prepared the menu. John, Henry and Leon set up a serving table in the back of the meeting place. John and Leon did the selling and Henry served as delivery boy between the kitchen and basement. We had never had such fun. We prepared ice-cold lemonade, hot dogs, hamburgers, cheese and sometimes cakes and pies and chilli. Then one night, one of the precinct brothers whispered to John, "say, don't you boys have something to sorta uplift this lemonade?"

"We are truly sorry, brother, the old lady would never permit that."

"Well then, I'll tell you what. Give me an empty glass. I'll put in a little foundation and then you boys can top it with your lemonade, all right?"

"Right," said John and Leon as they nudged each other in the side, and turning to Leon, John said, "now little brother, that's a story we will keep to ourselves, right?" "Right." Before the evening was over, all of us knew about it except mother Sarah.

"My goodness, they sure do like the lemonade," exclaimed Sarah after the first week. "Tomorrow, buy a couple of dozen more lemons. Get a dozen oranges, a little orange juice added will make the colour richer. And Ruth, make it a little stronger.

We don't want them to think that we are trying to
make too big a profit from them. Everything went
perfect. Everyone was happy We had never had it
so good. Finally came the week of the election. First,
Mr. Jones and then Mr. Ellis asked Sarah to work
on the streets, distributing voting paraphernalia the
day of the election. Sarah accepted both offers.

"The Bible says, you can't serve two masters at
the same time," cautioned Lula.

"Who said I'm trying," asked Sarah. Truly, all
of us thought that now Sarah was in "over her
head." We could not figure out how she could work
for two different political parties in the same block,
on the same day, without being discovered. But we
had under-estimated Sarah as a strategist.

First, she took out her winter overcoat with the
large lapels and the extra wide collar. Lucky for
her, it was cold in Chicago that November day. On
the top of her lapels, she penned the Democrat's
badges, lists of candidates and buttons. She figured
that in such weather, her coat would be fastened
up and no one would see her democratic trappings.
She placed her republican riggins under her lapels.
When she met her neighbours on their way to the
polls, she said to each of them, "Now, I know I
don't have to tell you how to vote." That simple
statement saved her from having to declare herself.
To us, she cautioned again and again:

"You all must be on your toes this day. You
know Mr. Jones and Mr. Ellis. And John, you and

Leon know most of the people who have been coming to the meetings downstairs. Most of them won't worry about what I am doing. But there is always one who will try to do everything the white folks tell them. Those are the ones you must watch. Go by the polling place so that you can see who is inspecting. All of you have your stations. If you have to leave your place, let one of us know and we will cover for you. Your job is to let me know if danger is approaching and from what direction." We felt as soldiers being ordered to our positions in battle. We pledged in our hearts that we would not fail mother. It was our family against the "system," what ever it was.

One thing that worked in Sarah's favour, she knew the occupants of every house on the block. She was a friendly soul. She was on speaking terms with every family. If both republican and democratic captain were near her at the same time, she would simply knock on the nearest door and say, "Sister, can I come in for a minute and warm my feet?" And that would be that. At the end of the day, she was tired, but she had won. We had won. We had for once in our lives, beat the "system." That evening, we sat down at a festive table of goodies we had seldom seen at the same time, broiled florida snapper, baked virginia ham with candied sweet potatoes, Turkey stuffed with cornmeal dressing and Lemon Cream pie for dessert. We felt as Paul Laurence Dunbar wrote, "Just like

new sausage, we were nearly stuffed to death."
When Lula started to talk about the morale
involved in her political activity of that day, Sarah
said in an even voice:

"Just shut your mouth and count your blessings.
We all know, without you reminding us, that what
we did today is wrong. But we must live. It should
not be necessary for us to do what we did today or
what we have been doing these two months. We
live under an inhuman system. There are a precious
few people in this world who care whether we live
or die. Tomorrow and for a few months to come,
we are going to be able to sit down and eat at a
table with decent food. The house will be warm all
over this winter. This is a working family, a hard
working family. But as hard as we work, we can't
make ends meet. We should be able to sit at such
a table whenever we wish. We don't sit on our
backsides waiting for the charity cheques, that's
gone before you can say, "jack-rabbit." The one
thing I would like to do is send those cheques to
that president sitting up there in Washington doing
nothing but playing golf, swimming and eating
whatever his appetite calls for and tell him to use
them for his toilet paper.

All of my life, I have worked from sun-up to sun-
down and after. All of you, instead of going to the
playground after school like other children, must go
to a job. You boys spend your time after school
going up and down dirty alleys, picking up trash

and old bottles to sell. You haul groceries or you pick chickens, wash windows all day on Saturdays. I don't mean to say its degrading. Any kind of honest work you do is honourable. What I am talking about is this; after you do all of these jobs, we pool our money and it is not enough to give us a decent living. And God knows that is not right.

"Yes. There was a wrong committed today. But the wrong is not what we did. And don't hate yourself for one minute. However, you must hate a system that forces honest, hard-working, christian people to do such a thing in order to live decently for a few months. And don't you think for one minute that brother Jones and brother Ellis and many of the others out there today didn't know what was happening. They just closed their eyes and pretended not to see. And both of them, although those old Democrats are as poor as church mice threw as much our way as they possibly could. And you must remember too, we are not the only poor souls in this neighbourhood. And they tried to spread their help around as best they could. And don't forget that those big shots down town only gave them crumbs in the first place. So I hope sister Lula, that these few words find you convalesing."

"Amen," we chorused.

"Quiet," pleaded Sarah, "I don't want to hear another word about the activities of the last two months." I felt that I was seeing my mother for the first time. I wanted to have such strength. I wanted to ease her burden. I realised for the first time how much she suffered in silence. I silently pledged that one day I would make her proud of me.

VII

Conflict and Confrontation

The excitement our family had enjoyed in the Election in 1936 had barely subsided before some of us were involved in another, equally electrifying. The black district on the Southside is called "Brownsville." Our churches were totally black. It was only at election time one might see a white representative from the Mayor's office who had been sent to beg for Black support for a candidate. Usually he sat nervously on the edge of his chair ready to run at the least provocation. It was really amusing to watch their reaction to some parts of the service. Sometimes the congregation laughed heartily at something the minister had said, while our white visitor was not quite sure whether he saw the joke or if he was permitted to laugh or was this just something among the Blacks. And so he turned red in the face and fidgeted in his seat.

Once in a while a white would slip, he thought, in at the back of the church or balcony and sit as small as he could. He had thought he would get by unnoticed because we have so many light-skinned blacks who could be white if they chose. What he had not realised is that the usher at the door had spotted him when he entered and had reported him to the pastor before the poor man had found a seat. He would be quite surprised to hear the pastor say when he rose to give the morning sermon, "I understand that we have a white brother worshipping with us this morning. Stand up brother so we can see where you are. The white brother would look very surprised as hundreds of eyes turned on him. And the minister would continue, "I want those of you sitting near this brother to shake his hand and bid him welcome, let everybody say amen. "Amen," the church would respond.

The schools in Brownsville were 99 per cent black. A few of the white teachers who taught in black schools permitted their children to attend classes in the same school. Howbeit, one could safely say that our district was almost solidly black, except for one thing. White businesses.

Up to that time, I had not noted this fact. We took things for granted. However, our eyes were opened in 1936. Chandler Owens, Editor of a radical magazine, The Messenger, and A. Phillip Randolph who served as one of Dr. Martin Luther King's strategist in the Civil Rights Movement of the 1960s and who was known as the "elder statesman" of Black labour leaders sponsored a little newspaper called, "The Whip." Its motto was: "Don't Shop Where you Can't Work."

Before 1936, nearly every business in our

community was owned by whites. Each morning they came in their fine cars, opened their shops, took as much money as they could from their black customers. At closing time, they put double and triple locks and burglar alarms on their windows and doors, got into their limousines and drove back to their fashionable homes in districts where Blacks, no matter what their status, were not permitted to live. Blacks cleaned the floors, washed the windows and carried out the garbage. Even on week-ends when business was "booming," these merchants brought in their teenage sons and daughters as extra help, instead of hiring unemployed members of the community. The "Whip" vowed to change this.

My brother Jack became a member of the planning committee at once. With the promise to "keep my mouth shut-just listen" I was allowed to follow him to these meetings. To our surprise, many came from our school. We soon found though, that we were much too radical. We were ready to burn the enemy out. The leaders were experienced men and women, so saner minds prevailed. They encouraged us to be a part of the movement. They organised a junior group which they called, "Social Action group." Our social action was mostly running errands and handing out leaflets in the district. But we did feel that we were a part of the revolution, for a revolution it truly was. We felt very proud as Mr. Owens allowed us to report on the reactions we had encountered. Even though some of our comments were childish, the adults seemingly took them seriously. We were proud of ourselves.

A group of school teachers posing as house maids, went into a number of white elite sections of the city to shop. They brought back proof that the inhabitants of Brownsville were paying higher prices for meat, butter, eggs and milk. Families in our neighbourhood who had only one light bulb hanging from the ceiling in each room were paying as much as whites who had table lamps, floor lamps, wall lamps and indirect lighting turned on just for the cosy effect and atmosphere.

Mechanics discovered that merchant-men who sold "weight" goods had rigged their scales so that their customers were losing 2 to 3 ounces on each pound of purchase. They revealed some grocers who were using rocks shaped like white potatoes. The "Whip" publicised these findings. This information was sent to the churches. On Sunday mornings congregations were admonished from the pulpit to "watch the scales, follow the hands of the grocer, see that only your goods are on the scales, see that the scale stops before your goods are taken off."

Several committees of labour union men and women were formed. These went into each store and shop asking owners to hire one or two people of colour, according to the size of the business. If they refused, pickets were placed on the side-walk in front of the store. The results were stupendous. A few of them refused and found themselves out of

business in a very short time. Most of them
complied. This idea of "Don't Shop Where you
Can't Work" spread to many black districts in the
USA with the same results.

I was one of the beneficiaries. I got a job working
in Woolworth's five and ten cent store on Forty
Seventh and South Park. The hours were from 3 to
6 on Thursdays and Fridays and all day Saturdays.
I was selling pots and pans in the basement. By the
time I finished High School, 2 years later, I had
worked myself to the "Notions" counter on the first
floor. My pay was almost double what I was getting
as househelp. I no longer had to crawl around on
my knees scrubbing floors. As Mahalia sang, "I
was Moving on Up a Little Higher." I was less
tired. My morale was boosted one hundred per cent.

Because of this job in Woolworths, I had more
spare time. Before, when my class had engaged in
sports, I was excluded because I had to work after
school every day in the week. Now I had some free
time. I was especially good in Basketball and Field
Sports. I was able to win a number of Gold medals
in High School City-Wide Sports competition.
Through these contests, I attracted the attention of
the Chicago Park District. The summer I graduated
from High School I was given a job as Supervisor
of the Children's Playground in Washington Park.
At the end of the summer, to my great surprise, I
was offered a permanent job in Madden Park. This
would be year-round employment. The pay was

good, but the hours were long – 2:30 to 10, five days a week. I cannot describe my feelings of security. I could now think of college. I would get a good foundation in music.

As much as mother had talked to us about the problems we would meet in the wider world, I was not prepared for the brutality of it. After I had worked in my new job for more than a year, I felt secure. I would definitely go to a musical college. I wanted a university degree.

Although my aim by now was to be a singer, I wanted something on which to fall back if I did not succeed as a singer. My mother and the rest of my family were with me in spirit, however, none of them could help me financially. I had to make it on my own. One June morning, I went back to Phillips.

Although Mildred Bryant Jones had been my music teacher for the four years I was at Phillips, I went to my chorus teacher, Aline Burke for advice. Mrs Jones was a product of Fisk University. Mrs Burke was an Alumni of the Northwestern University School of Music which is located in Evanston, Illinois, one of the suburbs of Chicago. Mrs Burke had talked to me about the advantages of going to N.W. Northwestern, one of the "Big Ten" among the Universities in the United States. A graduate from Northwestern holding a degree in Music Education was eligible to teach in the Elementary

School classes and High School Music in any town in the USA.

True to her word, Mrs Burke promised to help me. She was glad that I had chosen her school. I was advised to write in for an application. She gave me a beautiful letter of recommendation which I sent along with my request for entrance. I felt that I was already there.

Can you imagine my shock when a few days later I received a reply saying that "the quota" for black students was filled for this year, but if I would apply for next year. I was sure to be accepted?

Upon reading the letter, Mrs Burke turned as red as a beet. She had praised Northwestern so highly. This too was a shock for her. I saw her eyes fill with tears. I turned away in order not to embarrass her more. When she was able to speak, she asked me to leave the letter with her. She would call Dean Beatty who was head of the music department. I had been swinging between tears of hate and indignation since that morning at ten o'clock when the postman had brought our mail. Over and over I thought of the hundreds of students admitted to that school, still only five could be black. And these five were forced to live with black families in Evanston. They were not permitted to live on campus in one of the many dormitories. My feelings as I left Mrs Burke was one of extreme frustration. That morning I had been hating everything white with a purple passion, but here was one who felt as badly as I about my situation. I could feel her compassion. How could I hate her? Two days later, she gave me a message from Dean Beatty: I could enter Northwestern in the Fall, if I would assume the responsibility of my living quarters. I accepted.

Northwestern was a beautiful campus located in Evanston, Illinois which was about 1 hour and 15 minutes by underground from where I lived in Chicago. The facilities were most impressive. I was especially moved upon seeing the practice rooms, a four storey building with hundreds of small sound-proof rooms with a piano in each room. The doors stood open. All free. I often wished that I could have been on campus long enough to explore it fully. God only knows what problems I would have had, if I had been around Evanstone for anytime. I had to be at my job at 2:30, so I had had to take early classes.

It was a hard four years, especially the last two. I had to be in class at 8:15 which meant that I had to rise from bed at 5:30 or 6 at the latest. Nevertheless at the finish in 1944, I lacked only three points of being an "A" student. I don't know which of us felt more proud, my mother or I, as I received my Degree, Bachelor of Music Education.

By degrees, I learned that Evanston was one of the most bigoted places in the United States. One day in rushing from the campus to my job, I went into Woolworth's Five and Ten Cent Store to get a quick sandwich. I took a seat at the counter, because I thought it would be faster. I suddenly noticed that the people who were coming in after me were being served. I called this fact to the attention of the waitress. She leaned forward over the counter and fairly hissed, "We don't serve your kind in here." I did not believe my ears. I was stunned for a minute. Afterwards I asked to talk to the manager. Sure enough, he came out from the back and asked me, "Whats the trouble?" I told him. Without saying a single word to me, he turned and walked back through the door out of which he had come. The two serving girls giggled with delight. The other whites at the counter acted as if nothing was happening.

I had heard of such incidents taking place in Alabama, Georgia and Mississippi, but this was Illinois. I had much to learn. When I reached my job, I wrote a letter explaining the incident to the National Association for the Advancement of Coloured People. I could not think of anything else to do at the moment.

The next event happened a week later. It was right on campus. I did not seriously wish anything. I was just testing. This little cafeteria was packed with students, all white. Again I sat at the counter and waited, and waited. When I finally got the eye of the serving girl, I asked for the menu.

"May I see your membership card?" she asked me.

"Must one have a membership card to eat here?"
I questioned.

"Yes," she stated, shrugging her shoulders. I
knew she was lying so I said:

"You mean to tell me that you have seen the
cards of all the people who are here now before you
served them?" She was silent and I continued, "Just
two minutes ago you served those two people sitting
there. I did not hear you ask for a card."

Silence. I noticed that the place had become
unnaturally quiet. I remembered that not a single
soul in the place gave a damn what happened to
me and no one who cared, knew where I was at
that minute. Our civil rights leaders had cautioned
us to always make such tests in twos, never alone.

As Mrs Burke had told me, a degree in Music
Education made one eligible to teach in the public
schools of Chicago. In the fall of 1944 I applied and
was hired, first as a substitute teacher. The hours
were from 9 to 3, five days a week. With these
working hours I had more time to give to my music.
I intensified my study of repertoire and languages
under private teachers. I resigned from my
recreation job. I was no longer a regular member
of the Senior Choir, only soloist on special
occasions. Also other churches began to use me
especially for oratorios. I became the leader of the
childrens choir. I began to take a few pupils for
private lessons. My music world was gradually

widening. A sort of break-through – at least that is what I thought it was – came to me in 1948.

For 17 years the Chicago Tribune Newspaper had sponsored a "Chicagoland Musical Festival" 1948 would be the 18th. This Festival was always held in August in Soldiers Field. Eighty to ninety thousand people could be expected to attend. But preparations began long before August. Singing contests in connection with this gala day was held in every nook and corner of the USA and Canada to find the best Soprano, Contralto, Bass and Tenor. Those who won the preliminary contest in their respective city or state were sent to Chicago to compete for the title, "Best" in their own category. I had won over 15 hopefuls in Brownsville the week before. Semi-finals and finals would be held in the Auditorium Theatre in Downtown Chicago. The winning contraltos from other parts of the USA and Canada were present, 27 in all.

It was 9 a.m. in the morning. Contestants assembled in one of the small rooms to draw "lots." I dipped into the bowl and came up with the number one. My heart skipped a beat. A grand old "prima donna" standing near by saw the look on my face. She understood my feeling at having drawn number one and she said to me: "my dear, you have a chance to set the pace, do it."

The arrangement committee had chosen, "O don Fatale" from the Opera, Don Carlos by Guiseppe Verdi and "Ah Mon Fils," from "The Prophet" by

Giacomo Meyerbeer. Luckily for me, Boatner had told me from my very first lesson to always practice my singing early in the morning. "If you can sing at eight o'clock in the morning, you don't have to worry about being able to in the evening."

This habit of early practice, paid off that day. It was exactly 9:30 when I began to sing. Some of us were allowed to sing the entire song. Others were stopped after certain points, at the discretion of the judges. I was allowed to finish the aria because I was the first contestant. Around two o'clock, we had all been heard. Fifteen of us were asked to report back at 4 o'clock.

We drew "lots" for the second round. I stood with my number, 13. I have been in love with that number ever since. Again some of the singers were allowed to sing through the entire aria and others were stopped at various points. After all of us had been heard, the judges retired for some minutes. Upon their return, they requested four of the singers to sing the second aria. I felt depressed for I was not asked to sing the second aria.

Again the judges retired. This time it seemed forever, but it was only about twenty minutes. Then the chairman announced: "It is the united decision of the seven jury members that the winning contestant for the title "Best Contralto" in the Chicagoland Music Festival of 1948 are as follows: Fourth place. . . . third place . . . second place. . . . and for first place, Ruth Reese of Chicago.

For a moment I was frozen to my seat. I did not believe it. Then a burst of applause filled the auditorium and the tension was broken.

The same "grand dame" who had said to me, "my dear, set the pace," now whispered to me, "I bet when sopranos hear your high notes they could cut your throat." I was flattered beyond words. I cannot describe my feeling of elation as I saw Herman Billingsley and Tom Theodore Taylor coming towards me with outstretched arms.

I cannot think of two people who have spent as much time trying to help young black struggling singers and musicians as those two. Billingsley was a choral conductor and music critic. Tom Taylor was a piano teacher and accompanist, one of the best in Chicago.

Hearing of me through his friend Edward Boatner, who was my first voice teacher, he had invited me to come to him for practice at any time. I could have gone to him much more often, but I was ashamed because he never took a penny from me. At the end of our work-outs I would ask, "How much do I owe," because he had almost always ran over a hour, he would say simply, "child, you don't owe me a thing, just sing." I told Boatner of this one day and Boatner said to me, "just go to him when he can take you and don't worry about money. Tom Taylor has no financial worries." However, I still felt that I was imposing. For the

Chicagoland Festival though I had gone to him practically every day for weeks.

As soon as I saw those two, I had to fight to hold back my tears, but it was impossible. T.T. as he was affectionately called, acted as if he did not see, said matter-of-factly, "I have ordered a table for four at "Steak Johns." Then I began to laugh and cry. I was so ashamed.

While he stood there, a white woman that I had never seen in my life handed me an envelope and walked away. I opened it and found 25 dollars with a card on which was written, "best wishes." There was no name. "Oh God" I muttered as I tried to hold back a trickle of tears that had now become a flood. Then I heard T.T. say, "girl, let them flow, its good for your eyes."

That gold medal meant much to our struggle in those days. Black men have won boxing matches since the time of Jack Johnson. The great Joe Louis will never be forgotten. Olympic greats like Jesse Owens, Ralph Metcalf are a part of history. Jackie Robinson is in the Hall of Fame. Louis Armstrong and Duke Ellington are Jazz legends.

But that morning in the downtown Auditorium it was different. It was not a boxing match. It was not a track meet. It was not a Jam Session. It was a singing contest. The repertoire was European Classical Music. There were twenty-seven contestants from all over the USA and Canada. There was only one black among them vying for the title,

"Best" contralto. That I had won, was a bit of a sensation on the Southside.

Looking back however, I cannot help but feel a little bitter when I think of what winning that contest meant to white singers. Their future in music would have been assured. At least they would have been given the opportunity. They would have gotten an invitation to sing for the Chicago Symphony Orchestra, a tour of the fashionable women clubs would be certain. But all I received was the traditional "Brunch" given by the Lion's Club for the winners. It would have been an open scandal if they had not held that for me. Lion's Club had been entertaining winners of the Chicagoland Music Festival at a "Brunch" for 17 years. Of course at this Brunch, I was expected to sing.

And much to my disgust, the leader of the Festival introduced me to the more than 500 guests present as Ruth, Marian Anderson, Reese. He meant it as a compliment. I suppose it was. But who wants to be a copy of anything. However, I gave them my most charming smile and sung both arias "O don Fatale" and "Ah Mon Fils" and two Negro Spirituals. Thundering applause. The only other black in the place was my mother, Sarah bursting with pride. After it was over, we took the tram car back to Brownsville. I heard no more from the Festival Committee, but the Music Critics at the end of the year in their "flash-backs" of musical events of the season, hailed Ruth Reese as the

"Musical Find of the Year, 1948'. (I should not have been surprised at my treatment. Robert McFerrin had won the contest some years before and he had received the same treatment).

That Fall in 1948, I gave my Downtown debut in Kimbal Hall. The much feared Tribune music critic, Claudia Cassidy wrote: "Ruth Reese, heard in Kimbal Hall last night may easily have a fine future. Her voice is a beautiful contralto of range and power. She makes an attractive appearance and has a way with an audience."

Herman Billingsley wrote in the Pittsburgh Courier; "Ruth Reese presented the most beautiful likeness of a dark goddess that I have ever seen on any concert stage. With her voice, stage personality and intelligence, Miss Reese can definitely become a name to be revered."

Felix Borowski in the Chicago Sun, Milton Edwards in Music and News, Grace Thompkins in the Chicago Defender all wrote in the same vein. Erich Liensdorf, the Orchestra conductor declared: "The voice is magnificent." I was very proud of these critics.

Now I was in a dilemma. I must choose between gambling on a career as a singer or holding on to my secure job as a teacher. It was impossible for me to say *No* to a singing career. I felt that I was born to sing.

I was advised to go to New York and decided to go for a short "look-around." Louise and Pat

Patterson, whom I had known in Chicago were now living in New York. Upon my arrival, they presented me to Anne and Leanard DePaur who were active in the musical life of New York. Anne arranged an interview and audition for me with the great singer and former Metropolitan Opera Bass, Leon Rotheir. Rotheir granted me a years scholarship. My study with him was interrupted only for two months because I had given my word to an impressario in Hayneville, Alabama that I would come to them for a concert tour. My first concert tour.

VIII

My First Concert Tour

Mothers with more than one child will hardly ever admit, I have found, that they have a favourite among them. So it was with Ma. The Sunday morning after I had won the gold medal in the Chicagoland Musical Festival, our pastor presented her to the congregation saying, "stand up, sister Reese, and let the people see the mother of our young black singing bird give sister Reese a big hand folks." There came storming applause. After the service members came to shake her hand. When they said, "you must be very proud of her," she responded as she always did upon being complimented for something one of us had done. Instead of saying, "yes, I am, thank you," she would say, "I'm proud of all of my children." I smiled to myself, for deep down I knew. When she whispered to me during the service, "Ruth, sister Miller Club would like to present you in a concert," I accepted even though I had other plans. Sister Miller was her best friend. I would let Ma have her moment. I would do a concert for the Willing Workers Club.

The organist and I were rehearsing for this

concert one hot August afternoon in the church auditorium, a week later. People were constantly passing back and forth, but I noticed there were four persons in the rear who sat during the entire practice. I will admit that we did "show-off" a bit. After we were finished, they came down to us and presented themselves. To my great surprise, one of them lived in Hayneville, Alabama, the little village where I was born, and he was Principal of the School. He came right to the point at once, "I wish you would come down to us and sing. I could arrange a tour for you."

Before Mr. Tennyson had mentioned the business arrangements, I had said, "yes," for I was truly delighted. And even after he explained that my pay would depend on "free-will" offerings, I was still happy. Of one thing I was sure. I would never be hungry on that tour. I had a host of relatives living there. We parted some minutes later with the assurance that he would contact me as soon as he could set up the tour. I promised I would bring what I thought would be a suitable repertoire. To my great surprise, he stated that he would like the programme he had just heard.

The programme, to which he had listened, was the usual sterotype concert programme consisted of Old English, Old Italian, Brahms, Schubert, Opera Arias and the customary group of Negro Spirituals. I did not agree with him, but I decided that if he wanted that programme, I would give it to him. I was overjoyed at being invited to come and sing in Hayneville, Alabama. I received glowing letters telling me about the preparations. We would have packed houses all over, he assured me. It would be the first time for such a concert in the places I would be singing. Established Black artists, who were under white management, would never think of coming to a place like Hayneville. The people had read about them and heard them on Radio. Their fees were too high for the poor people for whom I would be singing. Some of them had been south, but had sung only in the capitals like Montgomery. Many of these places, black people were not allowed to enter. My concerts would be held in churches and schools. My first concert would be in my mothers family church, Mt Moriah.

I arrived one week before my first concert wearing a brand new luxurious, genuine grey persian lamb fur coat. No one had bothered to mention what kind of weather we would be having in Alabama in January and February and I had not thought to ask. I missed many a meal in order to save money for that coat. I felt that that coat was a part of my flesh and blood. I had been determined to have a real fur coat. I had had only one other piece of fur before I bought this coat. I had owned a silver fox scarf. I will never forget my embarrassment one late summer afternoon as I stood talking with three of my sorority sisters, when one of them stooped and picked up something from the sidewalk. It was the tail of my fox scarf. She handed it to me asking, "is this yours" I was the only one wearing fox. Each of them were wrapped in a jacket or stole of baby mink in various shades.

After that vexing experience, I had decided that my next venture in fur would indeed by cautious. As a result I was very elegant, but uncomfortable in that balmy Alabama weather as I descended from the train. Mr. Tennyson greeted me with the words, "welcome to Alabama, we are having lovely weather, I'm afraid you won't be needing that coat down here." I refused to part with it. I wore it draped over my shoulders the whole tour.

Hayneville is only about 10 miles from Montgomery, but Mr. Tennyson took a round-a-bout route. He wanted to talk to me before reaching the village. "Now, Miss Reese," he began, "I hope you fully understand our situation down here. We do not like it any better than you, but we live here and we will continue to live here. So we must try to get along with these people, if we can. All of us know that its different "up North." These people here do not like it. First, I will take myself for an example. I can get anything I need from them. I can get my car renewed before many of the leading white citizens, because I act a certain way. I hope that you will try to grasp this fact and will not make trouble for those of us who will be here after you are back in Chicago."

I assured him that I would be a "good nigger"

the two months that I would be in Alabama. We discussed the relative conditions of blacks North and South. For some reason one has always had the illusion that blacks in the North are so much better off than their brothers and sisters in the South. However, I did not argue the point for I was nearing my first test. In the station in Montgomery I had told Mr. Tennyson that I would like to stop on the way to my living quarters and buy some fruit. As long as I can remember, it has been a habit of mine to take fruit with me when I travel. I suppose it has something to do with an insecure childhood. I have always had a desperate fear of being hungry.

"We will stop in Mrs. Bright's store," he told me. "You can buy all you need there, I think." The store looked typically American. One could buy everything from a radio to a kitchen sink. I wondered as I entered if it was the same store my family had used when they lived there. There was no time to ask. We were getting out of the car. As we entered the store, I very nearly burst out laughing, for here before my eyes I was witnessing a perfect performance of what we call an "Uncle Tom."

Albert Tennyson was a tall, handsome, athletic looking man. He had earned his Master's Degree in Education at Colombia University in New York. When I met him for the first time in Chicago that warm August day, he had been attending Summer

School at the University of Chicago where he was working on his Ph.D. in Education. He was Principal of the Central Training School for blacks in Hayneville. When Mr. Tennyson walked into that little general store, the transformation he made upon entering the door, was startling. I watched fascinated.

At the moment, it was both amusing and sad. I was very happy that he had prepared me. However, I was not fully ready for what I saw. First, he took off his hat as he entered the door. There were two people in the store. A middle-aged woman was serving a stooped-shouldered white farmer who had on a pair of dirty worn over-alls. His sweat stained straw hat was pushed back on his head. I registered that fact immediately. He was buying cotton seed. While waiting for him to finish, I glanced around me. The smell was delicious, with peppermint candy, oriental spices, pickled cucumbers, onions and garlic. Finally it was our turn. Mr. Tennyson slowly approached the counter in a somewhat bowed, meek manner and said.

"Good evening, Mrs. Bright." Mrs. Bright had nothing to say about the weather, whether it was good or bad. She did not return his greeting. She simply looked over at me and said: "That's the girl that going to sing here?"

"Yes, M'am," he replied. Of course I was all smiles as I thought to myself that I was rather tall and old for a girl. The dear lady did not say one

word to me. After a slight pause, Mr. Tennyson
continued, "Mrs. Bright, Ruth here would like to
buy some fruit." Now up to this time, I had been
Miss Reese, but now I was plain Ruth. His English
was no longer Colombia University. Mrs. Bright,
on the other hand had not changed. She exhibited
the same attitudes that had been nursed and
handed down through generations of her forebears.
Tennyson to her, was just another black boy
standing there with his hat in his hands. After she
had kept us waiting for some minutes, she seemed
to remember that we had come in on business. At
once, she began that "baiting" that I had heard
blacks talked about so many times. She was fishing.
Indeed, she was angling for two small words from
a black. Those words were "yes" or "no." The
most important and significant thing for her at the
moment was whether this black "girl" from
Chicago would dare use the simple words, "yes"
and "no" to her.

I have never before or since had so many questions put to me in so short a time whose answers
could be yes or no. The poor woman had under-
rated her target. My mother had schooled us well
in the evasion of these words. When we entered
the schools in Chicago, Mother gave us definite
instructions. "When you are asked a question that
requires "yes" or "no" for an answer, you must
answer, "Yes" or "no" and never add "m'am" or
"sir." And if I hear one of you saying "yes, m'am"

or "yes, sir" to any one black or white, I am going to whip your backside until you won't be able to sit for days. You hear me?" We heard and we remembered. I was very happy that Mr. Tennyson had prepared me. It is very difficult to carry on a conversation even with friends or when you make a game of it as I heard once, without answering Yes or No. I came through my first test with flying colours, and Mr. Tennyson was pleased. When we emerged from the store, he was again the candidate for a Ph.D in Education and I had retained my Miss Reese status. I had to ask him how it was possible for him to switch roles so fast and he answered:

"Child, I have a school to run and it is the only school black children have here." There was no need for him to say more. I understood. I too, had probably used the words "Uncle Tom" too readily.

When I met Tennyson the next day, he was all smiles. "Ruth," he said, "You have really won them over. I was in Mrs. Bright's store today when Mrs. McQuorter came in. The first thing Mrs. Bright said to her was, "you know that girl came into my store yesterday to buy some things and not once did she say yes or no to me." We both laughed heartily and then we shook our heads. What poverty, we thought.

On my second day in Alabama, Mr. Tennyson drove me over to see my family's former homestead. We stood there in silence for a while. Tales I had heard my mother tell came back to me. Mr. Tennyson must have sensed my thoughts for he said, "Well, it's nothing like it was when your family was here. No one has lived here for a long time. You can see how they have stripped the place. Almost everything has been carried away. All the old McQuorters are dead, but the family still owns the place. However, when the people around here need kindling wood, they just sneak up during the night and tear down a part of the building. Your father owned all of that good bottom land," he said pointing. "But I guess you have heard that story. There is no need for me to rake over the coals."

Maybe he was right. There was no sense in "raking over the coals," but the scene forced itself upon me. I could see mother as a child crouching in the stable loft with her brothers and sisters, while the animals moved about restlessly down below. She had repeated the story so many times of how our grandmother fearing the mob of white-hooded klansmen would come to the house, had taken them to the hay loft to hide. In the dark they lay, feeling each others cringing, trembling bodies. "Don't make a sound" grandmother had told them. From the sound of her voice, they knew that she was shedding silent tears for her two sons, who had been hanged the day before, because they had dared to ask the white boss, after working three weeks, for their pay. Never again could she hear Robert's jovial "hey, Mom, what's cooking in the pot?" Or

Joe's answer, "lie-row, catch medlo, that's what."
I remembered as mother used to tell us this story
she would seemingly forget our presence. As we
looked into her sorrowful, bitter face, we heard the
mob, we saw the smoke, we smelled the burning
flesh and we swore that when we grew up, we would
kill all of the white folks in the world. A cough from
Mr. Tennyson bought me back to the present. We
drove over to see his school.

Would you believe it, the building that housed
the "workshop" had mysteriously burned down a
month before. Again I was reminded of my mothers
stories of how my father, along with other farmers,
felled trees, split logs, worked half the night to help
build Central Training School, only to have it
burned down after two or three years. She had told
of how she and other women in the community
baked pies, sold cookies, held bazaars in order to
raise money to buy equipment. Yes, the Work-Shop
would be rebuilt. We continued our sight-seeing
tour.

We drove through long stretches of land with
tall pine trees. Tennyson pointed in passing to a
dilapidated white house, "Old Mrs. Owens lives
there. She owns all of this, but she does not know
that, she has been crazy as a betsy bug for years."
After a while he said, "now we are coming into
government-owned property. Negroes are not
allowed to buy. We can rent, but not buy. There is
a gentlemen's agreement not to sell to blacks." I

would hear more about such things later, when Tennyson was sure that he could trust me fully. I would be let in on secrets that thrilled my very soul. Howbeit, Tennyson warned me again and again about discussing the black and white problem with people I would meet. "When there is a third person present, you must not say one word about colour not even to me." I slipped up only once.

Our pianist was unable to follow us for a couple of days. There was no telephone where I lived so Tennyson and I went over the road to the home of a neighbour. She fairly oozed with hospitality. While sitting there, I remembered the fantastic white Music Conservatory of Music we had passed on our tour. Without thinking, I blurted out, "Mr. Tennyson, what would be the reaction at that Conservatory of Music if you called and asked them for a pianist?" Silence. Dead silence. My question was loaded with social implication. I had implied race mixing. When Mr. Tennyson spoke it was about something wholly irrelevant. This event took place about 11 o'clock in the morning. When I saw Mr. Tennyson at 4 o'clock he told me that the Superintendent of Education had called him to his office at 2 o'clock that day and had asked him, "What kind of a trouble maker have you brought into this district?" Needless to say, the Superintendent was at the first concert. It is impossible for me to describe my loathing of that woman. To have to watch "them" and "us" is a terrible strain. So came the day of the first concert.

I had insisted upon coming to the locale nearly two hours ahead of time. I arrived just in time to see a team of four oxen pulling a wagon, upon which sat four husky men and a piano. How I longed for a photograph of that scene but I was afraid I would offend if I had asked to take a picture.

When I entered the church, the cultural committee was busy sewing white bed sheets on rollers. These sheets would serve as curtains for the stage. At the back of the stage, one sister was busy coaxing a little black pot-belly stove trying to raise enough heat so that I would not be cold when I shifted into my costume. Mr. Tennyson had said that he wanted everything like Carnegie Hall in New York. So I had had Clotild Dent, a fantastic dress maker, create a model for me in red velvet that was absolutely "smashing." Tennyson had said, "Walk out on the stage at the stroke of 8.00." As I stood waiting, I could hear the murmur from the church and knew that the house was packed. However the sight that greeted me, when that curtain opened un-nerved me for a second.

Tennyson had told me there would be a goodly number of whites, in fact he had said it would be something of a record attendance for whites at a coloured function. In my excitement, I had not given it much thought. I had come to Alabama to sing for my mother's folks. I never dreamed that I would have a white problem on this tour. But the sight that greeted me when that curtain opened floored me for a moment. I was looking into the faces of eight fully packed centre front rows of pale faces. "Well I'll be damed" I said to myself as I tried to recover from the shock. When Tennyson had told me I would have a number of whites at the concert, I had not even thought of seating arrangements.

Suddenly something Lawrence Winters, one of our bass singers who suffered under the shadow of Paul Robeson had told me, came to mind. Winters too, had been greatly influenced by Robeson's stand on human rights, so he had stipulated in Nashville, Tennessee that he would not sing his concert unless he was assured that black people would be allowed to hear him. He got that assurance. When Winters finished his first song he heard strange noises at his back. Upon finishing the first group, he found that blacks had been seated on the stage with a curtain drawn so the audience could not see them. Two weeks later in Montgomery, Alabama, having learned from Nashville, Tennessee, Winters told the concert manager that he wanted blacks in the Hall where he could see them. This time he noticed that the white peanut and candy venders had been replaced by blacks. Winters remembered that he had said, "I want to see them, while I sing."

I recovered as quickly as I could after seeing this seating arrangement as I noticed that my white public was applauding as furiously as the blacks surrounding them on all sides. I admit, I felt a little sad when I saw that my mothers, brothers and sisters had been shunted to the side. There sat my mother's oldest brother, Abe Hunter. Abe Hunter was something special. He was singing Negro Spirituals before white America had heard of them. His unique method was delightful as well as instructive.

When he felt like leading a song, he went through a regular routine that never varied and the congregation never rushed him. First, he began to sway from side to side. With his left foot, he kept up a steady tap on the floor. With his right foot, he did a heel-toe-heel-toe pat. He clapped his hands on two and four rhythm. Here before our eyes, we saw an African Drum Orchestra embodied in one man. When Uncle Abe had set his tempo, the congregation joined him clapping their hands and patting their feet. And when he called out, "Ef you wanta go to He'ben, Lawd," the response was spontaneous and right on the beat as the congregation answered, "Plum the line, to see that bleeding lamb." Slaves brought to America were not permitted to bring their drums and other African instruments with them. But Uncle Abe and many like him, had their instruments in their souls. And from those beating hearts, the world has been given Negro Spirituals, Blues, Ragtime, Jazz and Gospel Songs.

Uncle Abe sat like an old Buddha and prayed out loud during the entire concert, "Lord, help this child, have mercy." My Aunts Lucy and Nelly sat beside him. Aunt Lucy is known in the family as the proud one. That night she sat as straight as a rod, clapping with her gloved hands. Aunt Nelly, on the other hand, almost jumped out of her seat. I am sure she would have come on stage to hug me when I entered if Aunt Lucy had not stopped her with, "you don't act like that at this kind of concert." My Uncle Elijah sat with his arms folded over his chest like an African Chief. Never have I felt such warmth before or since at a concert. The church was packed. People were lined up around the walls. Windows were opened and people stood outside and looked in. As far as I could see through windows, there were people. There was no need for that pot-belly stove smoking in the back.

Mr. Tennyson had told me to "knock them cold" with my first number so I had started with the aria, "O don Fatale" and Verdi's opera, "Don Carlos." They had not understood a single word of the text, but I thought they would never stop clapping, waving fans and handkerchiefs, shouting "amen and Halelujah." Aunt Nelly stood up crying like a child. I had to struggle with myself to keep from joining her. By the time I came to the Negro Spirituals, it was like an old-fashioned revival meeting. I had not agreed with Tennyson about the repertoire, but he proved to be right. After many encores, the concert was over. I was faced immediately with another problem that none of us had thought to discuss.

Our "special guests" were moving towards me, all smiles. I asked myself, "what in hell must I do now?" In the mood I was in it was difficult not to reach for their hands as they told me how much they had enjoyed the concert. I have often wondered what would have happened if I had reached for one of those white hands. However, I remained a "good nigger." I grinned from ear to ear. I felt both sad and frustrated as I noticed how patiently my black brothers and sisters were waiting for the "guests" to get out of the way. But the southern custom had to be served. After the last one had greeted me, that black flood of goodwill surged forward. I have never been hugged and kissed so much after a performance. Aunt Nelly was the first to reach me. Uncle Abe was doing an African jig. Uncle Elijah just stood and worked his head up and down like a yo-yo. We had a real fellowship meeting of cousins, and cousins and still more cousins. My First Concert Tour had begun. It was a fantastic experience for me.

In all, I did 32 concerts in small and large places, most of them in churches and schools. Many of them had never before heard a classical concert. Every place was a grand fellowship. It was a glorious experience for me. The tour ended in Hayneville where it began. The community would say good-bye to me at a party at the luxurious home of one of the prominent physicians, where I would meet doctors, lawyers, teachers, social workers, business people and community leaders. Some would be coming as far away as Birmingham, Selma and Montgomery. In other words, all of the elite would be present. The black elite, I mean. There would be no whites at this function. For blacks and whites to meet socially was absolutely taboo, that is, in the open. Again Tennyson warned me, "you must not say the words 'black or white' or up North or down South."

"I will present you to some of the people you have already met. Just act as if you have never seen them before. There will be some sheep and some goats and some jack-asses at this party tonight, but you do not know one from the other. Even if I say something on the race question, don't you utter a word."

I followed his instructions to the letter. The evening was spent listening to music, recitations and speeches on how much progress was being made in Alabama. There were a number of competent artists present. We are truly a rich people. Although nothing was said at that party about political action, I knew that the community was pregnant with political activity.

I was really proud of them. After Mr. Tennyson understood that he could trust me, I was privileged to sit in on a number of strategy meetings. If the news of such meetings had been conveyed to the white folks, I might have witnessed a lynching myself before leaving Hayneville, Alabama in 1949. For what Dr. Martin Luther King Achieved in 1955 and after, the foundation was laid by the people I was face to face with that night.

I felt sad that they had to keep much of their mode of action hidden from black people. Still I was happy to see and know that they had no illusions about their status. One can seldom encounter a black living in the North, who will admit that he enjoys only second-class citizenship. I found out during my tour, that my southern brothers and sisters knew exactly where they stood, what they wanted and were working to get it even though they had to do it "under-ground." I never tire of the stories I heard of these courageous people. There was one that I loved retelling when I came back "up-North."

It was the story of Howard Kelly. Kelly was generally known as a "budding" Uncle Tom because of the way he acted around white people. Kelly was a graduate of Howard University. He had majored in Political Science. Whites loved him because as Mrs. Bright had described me to Mrs. McQuorter, "he never once said yes, or no to a white man," without adding "sir." Howbeit, they did not love Kelly enough to allow him to register and vote in an election. Dubious means were used to keep black people from registering and qualifying to vote as, Pole tax, some were asked to translate

Chinese, some where asked to produce evidence that their grandfathers had voted. In Kelly's district, blacks were asked to recite the constitution of the United States. I doubt if any lawyer on the Supreme Court Bench could fill that order.

When "Uncle Tom" Kelly went in and applied for his application, he was ordered to recite the constitution. Kelly stepped back, made a military salute, placed his right hand over the region where his heart should be and began reverently. "Four score and seven years ago, our father brought forth upon this continent a new nation, conceived in liberty and dedicated to the proposition that all men are created equal. . . ."

As every child who has been to High School in America knows, this speech is required reading. It is President Lincoln's address at the dedication of the National Cemetery in Gettysberg, Pennsylvania, November 19, 1963. Students had to memorise this speech as part of their final examination. When Kelly had finished reciting, the two red neck, tobacco chewing gentlemen leaned back in their chairs and one said to the other, "he said that thing, didn't he?" Kelly was given his application form. However, if those two had known that the words were those of that Northern "devil of a Yank," Abraham Lincoln, poor Kelly might have been hanged.

Kelly became an elocution teacher. He rode his old brown mule from house to house giving lessons in dramatic reading. There were some homes he frequented regularly late at night. These were farmers of voting age. The lessons he gave each one was the same, Lincoln's Gettsyburg Speech. When later they went into the voter's registration office, hat in hand, and was told to recite the Constitution of the United States, they would straighten up, salute and begin Lincoln's address. In this way, a few of them were able to exercise their God-given right to vote.

I was told stories of this same Kelly joining the Ku Klux Klan. In his Klan uniform made from one of his wife's bed sheets, he did not look any different from the Judge, school teacher, police, doctor or politician sitting next to him discussing, "what we should do with these "niggers." Because of Kelly's presence in those meetings, many plans the whites had made for the black community, were thwarted. Whites were surprised, many times, that their intended victims had "flown the coup." How? Where? No one knew.

I said my final good-byes for the time being. After being around these blacks for some two months, I left Alabama with a firm conviction that if the black people of America ever won their freedom, the leadership had to come from our brothers and sisters in the South. Time has proven me right in this. For months after my First Concert Tour, I heard glowing reports of the effect the tour had had. And my heart sang.

IX
Paul Robeson and
Lawrence Brown

I was a little wiser politically as I left that warm, balmy Alabama weather. I spent a few days in Chicago reliving the tour with my family and then took a sad good-bye. My mother took it especially hard. Her health had began to fail. The years of hard work had began to take its toll.

It proved to be my last meeting with her. I understood her. She had worked arduously to hold the family together after my father passed. Now, she said, I was breaking it up. Other sisters and brothers had married and had left the homestead. However they were still "in calling distance." And she saw them every Sunday at church, or they could stop by and see her on their way home from work.

On one thing they were all united: I was making the mistake of my life in giving up a secure job to gamble. In the end, they wished me luck and bade me keep in touch.

A number of letters and a package had come

to me while I was singing in Alabama. The most interesting was the package. The Harry T. Burleigh Music association of South Bend, Indiana had plans to produce Clarence Cameron White's Haitian Opera, "Quanga." The violinist, Clarence Cameron White had travelled to the Caribbean and listened to the Folk Music of the islands, and had written music for chorus, orchestra, dancers, singers and three principal soloists. The theme of the Opera was Dessalines black troops' fight against Napoleon to free Haiti. It was very dramatic. The package that I had received contained the score.

The Association wanted me to sing the contralto part of Mougali, High Priestess of the Voodoo. I loved the part. The Baritone-Tenor, Fritz Vincent would sing Dessaline and Carmen Malebranche would sing the Soprano. The two had already said, "yes." They were waiting for my answer. This would be my first experience working with the exotic Caribbean rhythms. I telephoned my acceptance at once, and dived in to study the part.

We gave two performances to a packed house. Although the critics raved, little happened after that because the Association lacked the dollars needed to follow up with publicity and all of the other paraphernalia one needs in order to launch a project in the United States. America was not ready for a black Opera. White's "Ouanga" suffered the same fate as Scott Joplin's "Treemonisha." Maybe fifty

years from now some one will produce "Ouanga."
I hope so.

In the meantime, the Pattersons had arranged
for me to meet the legendary pianist, Lawrence
Brown. I had seen and heard him and Paul Robeson
in concert. Now I would meet him face to face.
Brown had been travelling around the world with
Robeson for some forty years. He knew the ins and
outs of concert life, so I counted myself lucky. Larry,
as he insisted to be called, was a well of knowledge
of Negro Folk Music and loved it. He was pleasantly
surprised when he discovered that I had brought
along several of his arrangements of Spirituals, but
I had always liked his arrangements because of their
simplicity. He sat down at the piano and we sang
his 'Motherless Child.' From that day, Larry began
to guide my singing career. It was in Larry's studio
that I met the great Paul Robeson for the first time.

I can hardly describe my feeling when he entered
the studio and subsequent meetings invoked the
same sensation. From the stage, he looked robust,
but face to face he was colossal. His booming, yet
gentle and velvety voice commanded attention.

When I met him the second time in the home of
the Pattersons, I sensed why the McCarthy
Unamerican committee was trying so hard to
destroy this black image. It was a revelation to me
to see and hear how the machinery of government
could be set in motion to manipulate the destruction
of one human being. He was dynamic. I was privi-

leged to talk to him a number of times. These talks were the high point of my stay in New York. My thinking about my music career changed. Not only me, but many black artists learned from Paul Robeson how we could use our art to help struggling people.

A year before I came to New York, Paul Robeson and the actor Canada Lee had organised a group called, "The Committee for the Negro in the Arts." The aim of this organisation was to fight the use of stereotypes in radio, the media, movies and especially T.V. which was relatively new. As Robeson explained, "The way the American movies have portrayed blacks and other minorities has had a far-reaching effect on the thinking of people around the globe. T.V. will be even more dynamic and impressive. The impact will be far greater and Negroes must organise to fight to see that the right image, a true picture is projected of black people."

I became a member of the organisation at once. Chapters were being organised all over the states. Blacks were alerted to watch for slurs in radio, movies and the media. They were told to report such findings to their respective chapters.

This committee was being taken very seriously. I was allowed to sit in on a meeting the New York chapter had with the Colombia Broadcasting System. The CBS officials asked for and received a list of "offensive" words and expressions like niggers, darkies, pickinanny, coons etc. Gee whiz, how many times have I heard friendly white people say that they thought such words as "darkies" were endearing terms. In these meetings, I met artists, Ossie Davis and Ruby Dee, Harry Belafonte, Sidney Poitier and many others.

It is good to reflect on the result of this committee. Its mission has been accomplished. One will seldom, if ever see an Al Jolson type of artist in American show-business, movies or T.V.

I must say, the seed of protest was planted firmly within me and I am on the constant look out for these breaches. I was sorry to leave New York, but I had to get on with my singing. After my success in the Opera, "Ouanga," Lawrence Brown and a group of artist friends had raised money for my music studies. I could debut in Town Hall in New York or I could go to Europe for further study. I chose Europe.

X

On Board Ship Europe Ahead

I left New York by boat for London in the early
fifties on board a ship belonging to the Holland-
American lines. A number of friends had come
down to see me off. The last thing Larry said to me
was, "You must learn to sing in the King's English.
Say hello to Madam Aldridge and Sir Roger Quilter
for me."

I stood on deck and waved to them for a time
until I saw them turn and go. It was my first time
on board a large ship. It was rare to see the American coast line gradually disappear. As we glided
passed the Statue of Liberty, my thoughts were
somewhat bitter. The Statue of Liberty – for whom?
Although I knew, because of my family, I surely
would be coming back, it was good to get away for
a spell. So, I went to my cabin to change for dinner
hoping to inhale a little European atmosphere on
board ship.

When I came to the dining restaurant, the headwaiter checked my name and then led me to a little
table near one of the windows. I had a fine view.
Being unfamiliar with the customs on ships, I had

made nothing of the fact that I had been seated
alone at a table. In fact, I liked it. I sometimes
enjoy eating alone, I can choose what I wish
without listening to my comrades suggesting "shall
we take this and then that" etc. And being alone
one does not have to enjoin in forced conversation.
In other words, I was perfectly relaxed at my little
table alone. But, unaware to me, a group of seven
young students travelling to Bulgaria for a Youth
Conference had started a "crusade" on my behalf.

I was surprised when I came to dinner on our
third day out that my little table had disappeared
and the waiter informed me that hereafter I would
be seated at table number fifteen. I thank God for
the sense of humour He has given me. I had to
laugh. I could have had faster passage on boats on
the American Lines, but I had wanted to get as far
away as I could from the American atmosphere.
Hence I had booked on the Holland line. But here
I was. I thought of Joe Louis's saying, "You can
run, but you can't hide."

The American aerial antenna was in evidence.
There were several meetings on board for "Americans only." In each of these meetings, a representative from the State Department lectured us on the
meaning and interpretation of the Marshall Plan.
He anticipated questions we would be asked and
gave us the answers. America, he said, is the
greatest exponent of democracy in the world. "You
must remember as you go abroad that you have a

splendid chance to help spread "the American Way of Life." I listened in awe. In my heart, I was hoping not only that "the American way of Life" would be confined to the shores of the United States, but that it would one day disappear from the face of the globe. There were long discussion periods. However I did not open my mouth, I did refuse to applaud – I don't know whether it was noticed or not. I had just left a milieu that was being hounded by McCarthy and his Committee.

So came our last night on board ship. At dinner, the captain had reminded us that "this is Carnival Night, everyone must come in costume – there would be prizes for the best, rarest and funniest costume." At ten o'clock the little dance band began to play waltzs, Polkas etc. and the characters began to stroll in. It was obvious that some of them had come prepared for this carnival, their costumes were so expensive and elaborate. I tried my best to get into the festive spirit of the night with my paper eye mask. Those of us who had come in earlier, kept a steady eye on the door for new comers. As nearly as always in these carnivals, some "minstrel" figures will find their way. But this one was unexpected by me.

One of the seven students, who had demonstrated against my being segregated in the dining room of the ship, came in black face. She could have passed for Al Jolson's pickinanny daughter. Her face was painted jet black with wide, thick, white lips and black gloves on her hands. She had a "nappy" wig with little ribbons tied all over her head. I decided to go to my cabin and get a good night sleep. However, I did notice that the next morning she had the decency to stay away from our breakfast table.

We landed in Southampton. In a few hours, I was in London for the first time.

XI
London

From Victoria railroad station, I took a little rare black box-like taxi to an address in Bayswater Street, where the student hostel in which I would live for nine months, was located. The house mother opened the door for me when I rang and showed me to my room. It was "nothing to write home about," but it was clean and roomy. The bed was comfortable. In one corner was a writing desk and a good reading lamp. In another corner was a little heating apparatus that ate shillings. My large window faced the spacious lawn of a former dowager duchess who had escaped from Russia during the Revolution who enjoyed feeding her daily visitors of seventeen cats. The toilet and bath were in the corridor. Howbeit my friends in New York had prepared me for the relative low standard of living I would be meeting. It was not until late September, though, that I discovered that I would have to continue taking my daily cold bath in a non-heated bathroom the whole winter. When I complained to the house mother she said, "Miss Reese, you are the only one taking a bath, the other students are perfectly satisfied with the jug of hot water that all can get in the kitchen." Brown had warned me, "when you are in a new country, you must adapt yourself to new manners and customs." So I did.

While unpacking, I switched on my radio to BBC. Immediately I heard, "Now we shall hear a number made famous by the nigger minstrels of –" I did not wish to hear. In the "what to see in London" column of one of the papers, I had read that Hazel Scott once the wife of Congressman Adam Clayton Powell, was playing at the Palladium. I would go to hear her. One of the first acts that greeted me was of a white comedian with a black stooge who ended the act by laying coal black egg. The audience roared. I wondered to myself if Hazel had seen the act and if so, had she done anything about it. For I had seen her in some of the meetings of the "Committee for the Negro in the Arts." I write here about only two incidents. In the nine months during my first stay in London, such incidents were frequent. I had reasons to write complaining letters to the BBC every week.

Lawrence Brown had arranged my study schedule in London. I was enrolled in the Oxford School of Languages for French and German. My voice teacher would be Amanda Aldridge, daughter of the great black stage actor, Ira Aldridge and his English wife. Miss Aldridge had had a successful career and had been teaching for a number of years.

She had been a prized pupil of the Swedish Nightingale, Jenny Lind. I was very happy to find that she would use the same breathing method-technique I had been given by Edward Boatner in Chicago and Leon Rothier in New York – the Yawn-stretch-open throat with emphasis on support. Sir Roger Quilter would help me perfect my English diction. Roger Quilter would have been a "His Lordship", if his twin brother had not pushed himself out of his mothers womb a few minutes ahead of him. However, he was the last to emerge and he had to be satisfied with being called a mere "Sir". He turned to music. I was able to add a number of his songs like, "The Crimson Petal", "It Was a Lover and His Lass", "Love's Philosophy" just to name a few, to my English repertoire.

Sir Roger Quilter lived in a luxury Villa in St James Woods. And he loved to entertain. He was a personal friend of both Robeson and Lawrence Brown. I soon understood that Sir Roger was somewhat a collector of famous people. In fact, Larry had told me before leaving New York that "you are very lucky to be accepted by someone as exalted as Sir Roger." Be that as it may, the hours spent with Sir Roger were quite interesting. When I met him, I tried to "put on" my best manners of behaviour. I tried to look pleased that one so high in his station of life had condescend to help an offspring of Abe Hunter, who was captured on the Gold Coast, West Africa and was brought in chains, maybe by one of

Sir Roger's countrymen. Sir Roger set a pattern,
that varied little, in our first meeting.

We spent most of our singing lesson talking about
his meetings with various Negro Greats. When our
lesson was finished, he would then invite me to have
a little "snack" before leaving. Quilter had picked
up the word "snack" from his American friends.
He did not seem to have the slightest idea of the
meaning of the word. Laughing he would announce
at the end of a session, "Now, we shall have a
little "snack" before you go, we shall take it in our
luncheon "nook". He then proceeded to lead me
into a room large enough to hold my hostel room
three times over. I tried to act as if this was a
natural event in my daily existence, but to be
honest, I had never seen such silverware except in
'Tiffanys' on Fifth Avenue, New York.

The dining table was about eight feet long. Sir
Roger indicated that I should sit at one end and he
proceeded to the other end. In the centre of the
table stood two solid, silver candle holders encasing
a silver bowl filled with fresh plucked flowers from
Sir Roger's own garden. The butler wore stripped
trousers and tails. His nostrils were always slightly
inflated as if he was smelling something or else he
had not had his adenoids taken out when he was a
child. He was there all of the time, but yet, he
seemed invisible until a glass needed filling. Never
a word passed between him and Sir Roger. I never
saw the cook or any other of the household help.

However, once or twice, I saw the whites of a pair of eyes peeping out from behind a drawn curtain leading to what I assumed to be the kitchen. Usually, I sent greetings complimenting the cook. I was careful to use the same language and the same kind of comments that whites had sent me by the hostess for whom I had worked. I was conscious that being a lady, I must not raise my voice too high. In my most charming English, I would say, "Sir Roger, you must greet the cook for me and say that this is delicious and that I wish I could have the recipe." And just as charming he would answer, "That I shall."

Then we would begin our "snack". Sometimes it would be Quail on Toast or roasted Quail. Another day we ate broiled Pheasant or Steaked Guiena Hen. I remember bowls of wild rice with Creamed Duck Livers. I recall Curried Shrimps and Wild Strawberries for dessert, or we sometimes had Glazed Pineapple or Brandied Cherries. We had proper wines served in the right glasses for each dish. These were only a few of the "snacks" I was served by Quilter. It seemed natural to linger at the table over coffee while he told me of his various meetings with famous Negro artists.

Some of them were just names to me then – Noble Sisle, Ebie Blake, Black Patti, Bert Williams. However, some of them I had met Langston Hughes, Brown and Robeson, Ellington. I had just began to delve seriously into black history with a

view to writing and so I was able to bring him up
to date on many of the names he recalled. This he
liked and enjoyed. But alas, one day Sir Roger
ended his reminiscences with the comment, "Ah,
the darkies, how I love them."

I let this remark pass without comment. He was
so happy over his charming little story, I did not
wish to spoil it. Well it was not the first time I had
heard the word, darky. I sat wondering how I
should handle the situation. I thought of Lawrence
Brown, Quilter was a dear friend of his. Would
Brown understand. What would he think. How
could I tell him. I sincerely thought Sir Roger
meant no harm when he used the word "darky" to
me. I did not wish to hurt his feelings by being too
sensitive. So I said to myself, "maybe its a slip of
the tongue. Then I thought, if its a slip of the
tongue, then the guy is false. In the end, I decided
to play it "cool". If it was just a slip of the tongue,
I hoped that he would not let it slide again. I had
only a few more weeks with him and I didn't wish
to spoil them. But lo, and behold, the very next
session he ended his telling with – "Ah the darkies,
how I love them – so like children." I was very
sorry, but pheasants or no pheasants, I felt I had
to bring him up to date. As kindly as I could I let
him know that.

"Darkies are dead Old Black done raised his head
Little black Sambo ain't no more And Old Jim
Crow gotta go." He accepted my criticism in good

grace. He had not meant to offend. In fact he seemed very interested in the changes. He wanted to know about the trouble Paul Robeson was having since I could give it to him first hand. My censoring of him for using the word, "darky" did not seem to make any difference in our relationship. He was as charming as ever at our next meeting and full of questions about our movement.

XII
Paris

From London, I went to Paris where I enrolled in a branch of the Sorbonne to continue my study of French and with the voice teacher, Felix Browdowski to perfect my French Repertoire. In London I had haunted the theatre, concert halls and opera. In Paris something new happened to me. There was something in the very atmosphere, something exciting. For the first two or three days, I simply strolled aimlessly. Once in a while, I would stop in one of the cafes overflowing on to the sidewalk and have a cup of tea. There were people of all creeds, colours and religions. It did not take me long before I found Afro-America. Meandering down the Champs-Ellysee one afternoon, I was suddenly confronted with a little, short black man saying, "Don't I know you. You are a singer from Chicago, aren't you?" Small world, I thought.

Yes. I knew him. It was Frank Rayford. He had also been a singer. Now he was living in Paris, working for an American family. At once, I sensed how anxious he was to show me how knowledgeable he was of what we, in our sheltered church life had called the underworld. Still, old habits are not easily broken. I was on my way to the Louvre. I was eager to see the paintings, "The raising of Lazarus," by Hentry O. Tanner. Tanner, I had been told, was the first Black painter to win recognition in Europe. One will find a reproduction of this masterpiece in almost every black church in the United States. I felt proud as I gazed upon his work hanging in this world famous art gallery.

After the Louvre, we just wandered about. Sometimes we stopped in one of the outdoor cafes just to watch the variety of people in their rare dress go by. Walking down one of the side streets, Frank said, "Lets stop in here for a minute." It was a cosy little cafe that is so typically French. One would have thought from the banter of conversation from one table to the other, that a family re-union was in session. While we waited for our tea, Frank pointed to a table in one of the rear corners. I shrieked, "Thats Richard Wright" and I was on my way to his table before Frank could stop me. I had never met Wright personally, but I knew Horace Cayton, his best friend. Wright seemed pleased when I told him that I had read his "Bigger Thomas" and he wished me luck when I told him I was trying to write.

That night Frank took me to a jazz club located in one of the many cellars of Paris. I heard Sidney Bichet and other jazz greats for the first time. I knew them only from their recordings. It was a fantastic experience to see and talk to them. Like many other black musicians in the 1930s, they had come to France seeking an outlet for their talent. Some returned to the States, but Sidney had stayed on in Paris. One will find a statue erected in Paris honouring him for his contribution to the cultural life of France. The statue honouring Sidney Bichet was erected long before the USA paid homage to Louis Armstrong and William C. Handy in like manner.

We came often to this cellar for "Jam Sessions." One night, encouraged by friends, I tried singing Handy's St. Louis Blues. I started off great, but when Sidney started cutting in with his tenor sax and one began to argue with me on his trumpet, I became afraid and stopped. Yet, from that night I knew I could sing Blues and Jazz. I had been singing Negro Spirituals since I was born. In Blues and Jazz, I was meeting the same blue notes. I was at home. All I needed was practice. I began studying Jazz Evergreens and the popular hits. John Logan a trumpeter who suffered under the shadow of Louis Armstrong, had also come to France in the 1930s. He was the leader of a 16 piece Jazz Band and a Cuban Band. I was overwhelmed one day when he called and engaged me to sing at a Gala his two bands would play for the famous Ali Khan. Here was my chance. It would be my first time to sing with a professional Big Band. The rehearsals went well. So came the day.

I must admit that I was nervous at the beginning, but after the first number I heard Logan say, "Well, all right then," I knew I was home, free. During my second round, I saw Prince Ali Khan approach the band stand and whisper something to Logan. While the public was still clapping, Logan asked me, "Do you know, 'Tell Me Why?' Take a minute pause. We will sing it." He told me later that Ali Khan and Rita Hayworth were dancing to that number when they fell in love and that that was his highness's favourite number. When the band started playing 'Tell Me Why,' his 'Worthy' was dancing with one of his four ladies of the night – the redhead. After I had sung a few bars, he stopped dancing to listen. At the end, he applauded. About ten minutes later, a waiter came to our waiting room with a tray of 16 glasses and a magnum of Venue Cliquot Sec Champagne, "Prince Ali Khan sends greetings and thanks for that number." It was finally over around 6 o'clock. Logan thanked us for a beautiful evening, "Food is on the Veranda, cabs will be waiting to drive you home."

We walked out to the veranda. The buffet table of goodies looked like the duplicate of one I had seen in a Hollywood movie of Emperor Nero's parties. The table was about 4 metres long. All the way down the centre were bottles of Cliquot Sec Champagne. On a side table were whiskeys and gins. The band went straight for the whiskeys. Touchy Grant, who was the male singer and also a student and I headed for the food and champagne. We were starving. We had been there since 10 o'clock. And then I made my first blunder of the night. I said out loud to Touchy, "Boy, I should have brought some shopping bags." Logan heard me. He whispered in a low but insistent voice, "Listen kids, at this kind of a party, you don't take food home. You may eat and drink as much as you like, but don't take anything away, you understand me?" "Oh yes" we replied. Then I whispered to Touchy, "Is he kidding?" "No," answered Touchy "He is not kidding, but you just watch me and keep your mouth shut."

So I did. We both began to eat and share a bottle of champagne. Every now and then, I saw Touchy look around slowly and at the same time he'd take a bottle from the table. Typical of me, I got the giggles in such a situation. Luckily for me, there was good space in my suitcase where my costume lay. By the time we had finished eating, I had stashed all of 4 bottles. I slipped away to the exotic fruit table and filled my portmanteau with tropical fruits. I noticed that as Touchy put on his coat he was bulging on all sides. We tried to stay as far away from Logan as we could as the band lined up for taxis. However, Logan kept running up and down like an old mother hen seeing to it that all of her chicks are safe. I had come out first and seated myself in the last car waiting for Touchy who would be going in my direction. When the car in front of ours pulled up where Logan was standing, Logan discovered that the occupants would be going in a totally different direction from where he wanted to go so he waved the driver on and said, "I'll ride with the kids."

"Dam," I heard Touchy say, "We gonna be stuck with that son of a bitch." Now, if Logan had gone to the front of the car and seated himself beside the driver, everything would have gone beautifully. But being polite to the last minute, he walked to the back of the car to hold the door open for Touchy. Touchy began to descend slowly to his seat. In so doing, one of the bottles in his left hip pocket fell to the ground. It did not break. Touchy sat silent, pretending not to see or hear. Logan was speechless with rage. With clenched fists he hissed at Touchy, "I told you. I told you." Logan was so angry he could not continue at Touchy so he looked over at me and said very sorrowful, "I don't know what you have." "Mr. Logan," I answered fervently, "I assure you that I don't have nothing." "I hope not," he said as he went to sit beside the chauffeur.

Touchy reached down and retrieved his bottle and passed it over to me and the car drove off. When Mr. Logan left the car he was too angry to say goodnight. Touchy directed the car to the hostel where most of our student friends lived. "We shall wake up the gang and have a champagne breakfast." It was 7:30. Touchy gave the concierge a bottle so that he would handle all the complaints about the noise we would make. We started on the first floor. We knocked on each door announcing, "Champagne is now being served as a compliment from his royal highness, Prince Ali Khan in Ben Mitchell's room." Ben was the only one of us students who had money enough to pay for a double room with a parlour and he had a piano.

To my great surprise, Touchy had brought along chunks of ham, a whole smoked salmon, a garb of liverwurst, fresh bread and eight bottles of Champagne. I was amazed. No wonder he could hardly move. When we were all assembled, we had a regular United Nation of Americans, Cubans, Russians, Germans, Czechs and Scandinavians. We drank from waterglasses and paper cups. It tasted just as good.

It was also in Paris that I discovered cabaret and the high cultural level it can attain. In a cosy little room, one could hear artists like Maurice Chevalier, Jean Gabin, Edith Piaf, and Yves Montand to name just a few. It was wonderful to experience these artists without a lot of paraphernalia and ear-splitting music one hears seemingly everywhere today. In Paris the "word" is cultivated and if you have not heard and seen cabaret in Paris, I am afraid you do not know what cabaret is.

One day Frank said to me, "I think I know a place where the Madam might like you. I have never been there, but I hear that it is a very "snooty" place." We decided to try it. We walked into the place around one o'clock one day soon after. It was a small cocktail bar, "Cinq A Neuf". It was a snug, cosy little place with expensive decor and as we found out later, a real "clip-joint". Madame Nicole, a former Music Hall Star, was sharp, but friendly. She took one look at me and said before asking me what I had thought to sing, "I will not have Jazz in my establishment. My clientel are the elite of France. They come here for cocktails before going to dinner or to the opera or ballet. They do not wish to hear Jazz." She stopped and looked at me. Without showing any sign of perturbation. I replied. "I have quite a repertoire of English, American, German and Negro Folksongs. I have songs of Brahms, Schubert and Hugo Wolff. I have arias from Handel's and Mendelsohn's Oratorios. I have opera arias of Verdi and Meyerbeer.

"What do you sing from Handel's Messiash and Verdi." When she heard, she answered, "Come in tomorrow at two o'clock, I would like to hear 'O Thou That Tellest Good Tidings to Zion' from Handel's Messiah and O Don Fatale from the opera Don Carlos by Verdi." Frank and I managed to keep a straight face until we were well away from Cinq a Neuf. We could not believe our ears. Handel's Messiah in a cocktail bar. Truly, we were shocked, but thats cabaret in Paris.

We were hired. Because I would be singing Handel, I was engaged for the three weeks leading

up to Christmas. I managed to hold the sophisti-
cated look in my face when she told me what my
salary would be.

Madame Nicole had strict rules that had to be
followed. Each artist would sing only two numbers,
no encores. We were a bit of a United Nation. There
were Americans, Canadians, French, Germans,
English, Spanish and Russians. Artist were not
allowed to sit with customers. We entered through
the back, did our bit, and left the same way. The
program was continuous up until a quarter to nine
o'clock. Madame Nicole would then in her
charming manner announce that it was near closing
time and invariably someone in the audience would
request a song from Madame. The routine was the
same every night. Madame said, "no", the audience
begged, "just one song". Madame would then close
the night with one of her singing-talking songs that
the French love so well.

Because of Madame's rules, I had no idea what
the prices were. Then one afternoon four of my
friends from SHAPE came to hear me. "Girl, no
wonder your pay is so good, this is the damdest
'clip-joint' I have ever seen," they told me when I
met them outside at 9 o'clock. We have just paid
20 American dollars for four cups of coffee and
toast . . . dam." Well, Cinq a Neuf was unique.
Usually cafes were places where friends met every
day. Seldom were they pressed to drink, drink or
eat and go. I soon fell into the same habit. I had

my regular table at Tom's Place, where I went
when I wanted to relax from my studies.

XIII
Miss D.

I had enjoyed my first cabaret stint in Cinq a Neuf
and was trying to find another, when I received a
call from an agent in Paris asking, "could you fly
to Copenhagen, Denmark at once, Katherine
Dunham is in need of a singer." Of course, I jumped
at it. Dunham was world famous. She had started
out to prove to the world that "the dance is an art
and not merely a movement of the hips or an outlet
for the release of sexual desires." She had studied
and researched into the origins of primitive move-
ments and rhythms. She had studied with Melville
Herskovitz at Northwestern University and she had
a Ph. D. in Anthropology from Chicago University.
As early as the 1930s, she was famous for her
interpretation of the Negro Dances such as the
Cakewalk, Strut and Barrelhouse Shimmy. She had,
without any help from other sources, organised a
company of 25 dancers, musicians and singers. In
15 years, they had travelled in over 65 countries.
She was a brilliant choreographer. I had admired
her for years. I could hardly wait to get started.

The company was holding forth in the The Oslo

New Theatre in Copenhaven. I was scheduled to
go on stage the last two nights. The pianist began
rehearsing me at once. Miss D. as she was called
by company members put in her appearance after
the third practice session. I understood that she had
been listening from the back of the theatre. She
welcomed me to the company and decided that I
deserved a press conference. At the press conference, I sang and members of the company danced.
After the press conference, Miss Dunham's Danish
agent whispered to me, "don't get stuck in this
group, you are too good, try going it alone." Of
course, I felt flattered, but at the same time I
resented his disloyalty. I was still enthused at being
there.

The evening of the same day, I sang my first
performance. The next morning, I was having my
own press conference. The Danish papers were full
of what Ruth Reese had said about the situation of
black people in America. When I came to the
theatre the second night, I saw on the bulletin
board, in large block letters, "No member of the
Dunham Company is allowed to talk to the press
without someone from the office being present." I
thought of the words of warning the agent had given
me the day before. When the company met the
next day, not one word was uttered about the press
conference and I refused to bring up the subject.
And so the press continued to seek me out. Whenever I could, I answered their questions. But usually

they were stopped at the entrance by Miss D's secretary or her husband and told, "sorry, Miss Reese is not available." When this did not stop my comment politically or otherwise, Miss Dunham called me to her office and there in an innocent and chauvinistic baby tone that she could bring into her voice when she was being an absolute bitch said, "I'm sorry, Miss Reese, but this company can have only one star and I'm afraid that that must be me. I hope you understand."

Well in the first place I did not consider myself as representing the Dunham company in my interviews with the press. And I did not see how my press comments about the unjust treatment of black people in America made me a rival for stardom in Katherine Dunham's dance group. I was sorry afterwards that I did not argue this point with her. I simply said, "Oh yes Miss Dunham, I am beginning to understand perfectly." She caught the significance in my "loaded" statement and voice for I saw she and her secretary exchange quick glances. She was waiting for me to say what I meant. I said not one word more.

It began to dawn on me that I had left Paris "half-cocked". There were many questions I should have asked before flying off to Copenhagen. In the first place, I found that I would be a member of the quartet, and that I would be supplanting the soprano, Mairiam Williams who had been in the company for 7 years. Luckily I have never had trouble with range, so that was no problem. I understood that there would be little solo work. That I could understand. After all I was joining a dance company. However, I had never given a thought to the fact that I would be "hemmed" in. In other words, I was no longer a free person.

I had been so pleased at being invited to join the Dunham company, I had missed some vital points from the beginning. When Dunham had welcomed me to the group in Copenhagen, she had asked Rosa Lee, the alto singer, to "show Miss Reese the ropes". Officially Rosa Lee began, "Anything you wish to know about this group just ask me. One thing I will tell you at once. We try to keep to ourselves." She meant of course, the singers. "You will notice", she continued, "That the principals keep to themselves. The dancers are together and of course you never go to the "head" unless you have been summoned." I chuckled to myself as I wondered who was at the head or tail and where was I in this class distinction.

Somehow I have never been awed by meeting humans no matter to what position they have attained. I respected Dunham who had been influenced by Paul Robeson as I had, for her quality of work and especially for her stand on human rights. She had made quite a stir, in the late 1940s by a speech she gave after her company had unknowingly danced for a segregated public in St. Louis. At the end of the concert, there were storming applause. She and the entire company assembled before the curtain and there Dunham announced, "We will never perform here again unless my own people are allowed to come in and see us." From that date, the State Department had been following her all over the world.

However, I was seeing more clearly that the public Dunham that I had admired did not "jell" with this private one. I would in time learn the private one. On our last night in Copenhagen, to the delight of the entire group, we read on the bulletin board, "the Dunham Company will go to Barcelona, Spain for the next two months." As the secretary explained, "we are going to Spain because the living conditions are favourable. The weather will be good. The food is cheap, but excellent. Hotels are reasonable. Dress materials are inexpensive. Sewing personnel costs are minimum. We will be in Barcelona for two months. You can relax. But remember one thing, no one must utter a political word while there. You think the jails are bad in America, but God help you if you get into trouble in Spain. Try to avoid the natives at all times." Miss Scott had said we were going to Spain to relax, that is if you can call rehearsing every day from 10 to 4 relaxing.

After a month, some of the costumes were ready and Miss D. began to call for dress rehearsals. I was sent to the make-up woman. She sent me on stage to get Dunhams O.K. Dunham took one look at me and said, "tell Rachel that you are too pretty." I gave Rachel her exact message. I pretended not to get the point of her giggles. After the second go, I was O.K. On stage Miss Dunham was building a scene around herself. One of the dancers sat-in for her while she and her husband directed from the audience. At first, I stood right over the "sit-in", then came Miss D's voice, "Miss Reese move about two feet to your left. I did. A second order came to move, I was then about one foot from the wings so I said, "Miss Dunham, I can sing this song just as well from the wings." And I meant that. If it was best for the show for me to be in the wings I would do that. And I had made my point for she laughed and said. "Miss Reese, am I that bad." One of her first directives to me when I went on stage for the first time in Copenhagen had been, "Miss Reese when I enter the stage, bring me on with your eyes." I took it all as part of my learning the theatre.

One thing that struck me as odd. I never saw Miss Dunham on bus or train when we travelled. I assumed that she had a private car. Then one day came the truth. It was at the end of October, but the weather was as hot as any day in August. Feelings were on edge. Not one of us felt like travelling on a second or third class train in Italy. As we gathered at the station Wilbur, one of the dancers announced with a bit of sarcasm, "my dears, Miss

D. and her entire retinue will "honour" us with their presence on this trip."

"Oh No!" broke spontaneously from members of the group.

"Yes love, there's no plane this time and to rent a car would be too expensive even for her "ladyship". Miss D's retinue consisted of Miss Dunham and her white personnel – the secretary, the maid, and the personal maid to the daughter of Miss D. I will admit I had wondered, what with all of the unemployment among people of colour, Miss Dunham had not coloured her staff a little. But that was her business. The lament that went up with Wilbur's declaration surprised me no end because I had gotten the impression that they truly loved Miss. D.

Later on, especially when they had had a little too much to drink, I listened to their confessions. Some of them over the years had been presented with opportunities for advancement, but Miss Dunham had sabotaged them with arguments of "duty to race," tears, gifts and dinner invitations until the chances were lost. One of the tenets in show-business and I am sure Miss Dunham is well aware of it is, "when opportunity knocks at your door, you take it for it may never knock again". I heard all of their confessions, but I was careful never to give any diagnosis. Somehow they knew that what they said would go no further.

On this hot October day, we were leaving Milano

on our way to Arezzo. The three last cars of the train were second class. The Dunham company occupied the last two sections along with Italian natives with all sorts of wares – chickens, vegetables etc. When we boarded the train, we knew we were there for a long ride so we had spread ourselves as best we could with companions who would be reasonably agreeable. What we did not know was that at Firenza the train would divide and only the last two sections would go to Arezzo. The rest of the train would then plow on toward Rome. After some time, I had to go to the toilet.

On my way, I saw something that if anyone had told me happened, I would not have believed it. Upon passing the last compartment, my eyes fell on the secretary scraping off the second class sign on the door with a penknife. I would not have stopped, but almost immediately I saw the maid with a small hand broom and dust pan sweeping-out the place. And then I saw the nurse maid actually washing the window-all of this on a moving train. I stopped. I stared. I was flabbergasted. "What on earth are you all doing?", I asked in amazement.

"We are cleaning a compartment on this train in case you do not see that," the secretary replied without smiling. I turned to Miss Scott and asked, "but why must you scrape off that sign?" "Well now, Miss Reese, you would not wish anyone to think that Miss Dunham would ride in a second class compartment on a train would you?" For a minute I forgot about my needs. I did a right-about face. I did not think that a living soul would believe. I wanted a witness. When I reached my compartment and told my story, I looked from one to the other. Not one of them budged. Instead they looked from one to the other with raised eyebrows and then Lucy said, "girl, you just stick-around-you ain't seen nothing yet."

After the help had finished cleaning we saw them go by with Miss Dunham's baggage. A little before the train divided, the lady herself sauntered in. She had been there for only about a half hour when the secretary came to each of our compartments with a request from Miss Dunham, "will the company members please use the toilet in the other coach." The others sat silent, but my answer is unprintable. I am almost sure that I was the only one who deliberately defied that order.

I find it hard to separate the artist from the person. I had worshipped the artist, Katherine Dunham. Now my eyes were fully opened to the person, Dunham. I felt bereaved. I was embarrassed. How could a woman of such brilliance have such a complex? I had to face the fact that the Dunham company was not the place for me. I said good-bye to them after the last performance in the Theatre National Du Palais De Chaillot on January 9, 1953. I remained in Paris to prepare for my

European Classic Music Debut which was booked for March 15, 1953 in the Salle Gaveau Auditorium.

XIV
Meeting Between Landsmen

I had just enjoyed a serving of Tom's "down home" barbeque and was thinking of how much better the barbeque at Lewis on 51st in Chicago would have tasted. I was waiting for the waiter to bring my coffee when my thoughts were interrupted by a voice saying: "excuse me, m'am, can I sit down for a moment." There was no mistaking that accent. It was Mississippi, Georgia, Alabama. It was saying: "can I buy you a drink, would you like something to eat? I hope you don't get the wrong idea, m'am. You see," and then he laughingly shook his head as if he had just thought of some unbelievable incident. "Please forgive me, M'am, but I have to talk about this thing. You see, I would not be here tonight if it had not been for two coloured guys. Yes sir, I would be dead" he said to himself. I thought to myself, here is another one of those "just converted Americans", but I said nothing. He continued:

"You from the states, ain't you m'am? You see, I come from a little place called Holly Hook, Mississippi. You know how it is down there, the coloured here, the rest over there. You never have much to say to one another. Well, you know, I joined up at the beginning of the war. Well sir, it was the first time I had been near any black person. There were two in our unit a guy called Archie and a little sawed-off guy called Duky. I had never said much to them. We all sort of kept to ourselves. M'am, you know how it is. You say you come from Alabama, then you know about these things. But I want to tell you before I go any further, its not like that anymore. Well sir, I would not be sitting here now talking to you if it had not been for those two guys."

He then proceeded to tell me the fantastic story of how Archie and Duky saved his life. The last thing he remembered, was that he had been wounded and was bleeding profusely. In their retreat, from enemy fire, Archie and Duky almost stumbled over him. He begged them to leave him and save themselves. "Beat it, you guys, just tell the folks that they got me."

"Those sons of bitches are desperate now", Archie told him, "They have stopped taking prisoners. They are just shooting every American they find in the ass." "But you know, m'am, I kept protesting and then I remember Duky saying: "shut-up, mother fucker, ain't nobody going to leave you here to die." M'am, I weigh 180 pounds. I don't know how they did it. Now, everytime I go on leave, I spend it trying to find those two guys."

It was a year later. I was in Sebastian, Spain singing with a group called "Harlem Melody". One free evening, I was walking down one of the streets in search of an outdoor cafe where I could drink a cup of tea. I came to an attractive place, but decided that it was too crowded. I was going to pass on when I heard an excited voice cry: "Excuse me, M'am, but didn't I see you in Paris about a year ago. "Oh no, I thought, this is impossible. But sure enough it was my soldier friend from Holly Hook, Mississippi. But this time he was happy. "M'am", he said, "You remember those two guys I told you about? Well I finally found them. They are right over there and I want you to meet them. He guided me to a table where there sat eight American soldiers, all brothers. I met Archie and Duky. One of his buddies said to me: "You know this guy? He is about to drive us crazy telling that story to every stranger he meets. Those 'ofays' from down home would like to kill him. He won't go out with anyone except us. We were forced to adopt him. Meet our white brother, Bill Evans. The ten of us sat at a table loaded down with Spanish wine and food. We sang Negro Spirituals until the wee hours of the morning. One could not tell Bill Evans voice from the rest.

When I first landed in Europe, I avoided white Americans. Just hearing the language made me angry. But I had finally rid myself of that burden for a tremendous burden it was. Now I was able to meet, talk and feel normal when I met a landsman. At last I was indeed free. Persons became individuals, regardless of colour. Recently, I had met a number of persons like Bill Evans from Holly Hook, Mississippi. I remember the cute, chestnut-haired brunette from one of the first families in Texas.

I walked into a party one evening. There she sat wrapped in the arms of a jet black brother. I had paid no special attention to them at first because this had become a common sight, especially in Paris, until I heard that Texas drawl when she exclaimed: "baby, I love you." That did startle me. I turned around and looked. Our eyes met. We were both thinking the same thing, what would happen to them if they were in Texas. Her next words proved me right for she said to me, "come on, sister, don't look at me like that. We are over here now where people are civilized and I do love this black boy. Do you mind?" Well, I really did not mind so I said, "carry on, sister. If little brother is happy, I'm hilarious, cause the sun do move."

I had been present a few days before in a group of American expatriates, all brothers and sisters. We had discussed, or rather they had discussed and I had listened. Coming from a sheltered church milieu as I had, I was naive about such facts of life. In the middle of our parley, a handsome brother who seemed to be about 40 years old, took out a bundle of letters. On the top lay one he had received that morning. It was from the wife of the mayor of one of the largest cities in the very deep South. She had paid his way to Europe. She had sent him money regularly. "Read it", he said to me as I gazed unbelieving. I picked up the one on top. Sure enough, she was asking him, "how is your money holding out?" She had written that he should meet her in new York on a given date. She gave the name of the hotel and the address. "I wish to do some shopping", she wrote. I looked up at him and reading my thoughts he said, "oh yes, I'll be there," and he laughed heartily. Yes, I thought to myself, the sun do move.

Heitor Villa-Lobos, the famous Brazilian Composer, had been impressed with my concert in Salle Gaveau in March and had invited me to his home on Avenue Victor Hugo, to hear some of his own compositions. You can be sure that I took time with my toilet that day. As a result I was looking very exotic. As usual, I was too early for my appointment. While I waited for Ben Mitchell, my pianist to arrive, I meandered up and down in front of Villa-Lobos' home.

Suddenly I saw coming toward me, tottering in her high heeled shoes, a little thick-set woman. She was wearing a veil over her tiny violet hat, set a-top her blue tinted hair. She had diamonds in her ears and sun glasses. Her face was made-up like a teenager. A blue purse hang from her shoulders along with that ever present camera. "Thats a coun-try-woman", I said to myself.

"Excuse me, Miss," she said as she stepped in front of me. Uh-huh, I thought as I engaged in my usual mental guessing game of where she came from, Mississippi, Alabama or Georgia. She was saying, "please tell me, Miss, where you got them shoes from. Dey look so comfortable. You see, I got bad feets *too* and the doctor done told me that my feets will never get well as long as I wear these kinda shoes." I smiled for I was thinking what would have happened if this meeting had taken place three years earlier and this woman had implied that I had bad feet. Instead, we had a very pleasant conversation. I told her where to find the shoes, the best store and the price. Then I marked her map showing her some spots she might enjoy. She thanked me, smiled sweetly and asked, "But tell me, Miss, where do you come from to speak english so good?" I looked her straight in the nose and said, Hayneville, Alabama, USA.

Her reaction was automatic. First, she was confused. Then she was infused with resentment. That sweet little made-up face turned tomato red. She stared at me angrily for a second. Then she turned abruptly and hastened away on her wobbly heels. I really felt pity for her, yet I could not restrain myself. To her angry back I called out, "God Bless America."

I puzzled for a moment over her reaction when she discovered that I was an American Negro. She could be polite and civil to a black from Africa or one of the islands. I realised that it was my exotic dress that had put her off. To be courteous and affable to an American black, was against the "American way of life. I had heard many stories of black men going South even in the 1920s wearing foreign head dress and being admitted to the best white hotels and restaurants.

It is a well-known fact that during the "Period of Reconstruction", the USA was on a definite road to become a real democracy. Howbeit, Big Business decided that blacks in the USA would remain the "under-dogs" in that land. And so, Europeans were recruited and imported to assure that the people of colour remained in the bottom position to which they had been assigned in the American society.

For a moment, I had been face to face and talked with a woman who spoke a southern dialect that indicated a lack of schooling. I had used a highly polished speech. Yet, she felt that her white skin had given her the license to pin humanity on a foreign black, while denying the same to a black fellow-countryman.

I had to struggle to throw her out of my mind as I saw Ben approaching.

XV
Italy

My friends really packed the house for me for my debut concert in Salle Gaveau. Some brother and sisters from the American colony and SHAPE had collected nearly fifty dollars for flowers and a gift for me. But they made one big mistake. They gave the money to Frank. They thought that Frank having been a singer and a frequent concert goer, would know the proper procedure. But, alas poor Frank was seeing lean days. He pocketed the money and went into the country-side to pluck fresh flowers for me. At the end of the concert, he came on stage with a big smile and handed me the biggest bouquet of weeds, I had ever seen. Madame Bouchenet, who managed my Paris concert, was standing beside me and she asked him, "what on earth is that" as she took them from me and handed them to one of the functionaries with a wave of her hand. I saw guilt in Frank's face as he sneaked away, but I did not know the facts until later that night at the party the group gave for me at Tom's. It was weeks before any of us saw Frank again.

The critics for the concert were surprisingly good.

I had them translated into English. A few days later, I spent a small fortune in newspapers, stamps and pictures. I wanted friends in the USA to know of my success. I knew Lawrence Brown and Leon Rothier would be pleased that I had proved a success. My sister Rosa wrote and told me how my mother took her copies to church, to the grocery store and showed them to every Tom, Dick and Harry that she thought had heard of me.

Since I had sung a classic concert in Salle Gaveau, it amazed me that critics had written so much about how I looked. Without any exception, they had all "dubbed" me, "The Black Rose". A few months later, a "Black Rose" perfume hit the market. A number of norwegian friends were surprised to receive from me a small flask of "Black Rose" the Christmas of 1957. When I did my first concert in the University Aula, I was happy that the company sent me a half litre of the Black Rose perfume. Since my debut concert in Salle Gaveau in 1953, I have used the rose as my monogram on my stationery and advertisement.

After the success of my concert in Salle Gaveau, I had expected requests to flow in or at least trickle in. Instead, my agent was offering me one entertainment job after the other. I was again reminded of the opposition blacks get when trying to break into the classic field. However, my funds were beginning to run low, so I had to think practically about things. And always in the back of my mind was the idea of blending music forms. My first job after Salle Gaveau came from Italy.

If Paris had been my school for cabaret, Italy proved to be my university for Revue. I had had a sample of it in the Katherine Dunham Dance Company. In Italy for nearly two and a half years, I was baptised in all phases of Revue from the smallest Spettacolo to the grand Hollywood style in Niagra Follies. I learned what it is truly like to interpret a song. Watching Callas in opera and Galluchi and many others whose name I have forgotten in Revue, I learned how to lose myself in whatever role I was playing. I learned how to "emote" like a native. I evolved from it all with a "Ruth Reese" style.

My first job was in a production called, "Harlem Melody", a musical fantasy in black and white. The clarinetist Benny Bailey and I were the featured persons in an all-Italian production. We travelled several months in Italy and Spain. When I went back to Paris, I found my agent bursting with enthusiasm. He had booked me with the American-Italian production of Niagara Follies for 1954, a 250,000 dollar Hollywood style extravaganza. I would be the featured woman singer. Rehearsals would begin within the week. So off I went to Rome again.

The show was built around a large portable swimming pool with a waterfall as background. When the elaborate lighting effects gradually went up the scene was breath-taking. There was always a notable gasp from the audience, as they got a microscopic view of the entire show. There were pretty girls in fluffy white dresses sitting in canoes being steered by handsome fellows in white tails. There were dancers gyrating on stage. There were swimmers and divers and stunt divers. There were jugglers playing their usual tricks. Accompanying it all was a 32 piece orchestra in full dress.

Suddenly the lights dimmed and a spot focused on me attired in a gorgeous creation in gold and jewels, as I sang, "I Wonder Why You Keep Me Waiting, Charmange, My Charmange." When we had been rehearsing the numbers I would sing in the show, I was reminded of Katherine Dunham and I chuckled to myself with delight, as I heard the producer order 8 tall, handsome dancers to "kneel as you bring signorina Reese on to centre stage with your eyes." At last I was a star. I loved it.

Niagra Follies opened in Rome where we held forth for two solid months. Then we went to Milano for six weeks, and then on to Firenze for two weeks. It was a very popular show. On the last night in Firenze, we were overjoyed to read on the bulletin board, "Company, attention! The Show Niagara Follies has been a tremendous successs. The show will continue as we follow the sun. Those of you who are unable to remain for another year, please let us know so that we can find replacements as early as possible. The company will travel in two days. Details will be given you tomorrow at 6 o'clock here.

You can be sure we did a fantastic show in Firenze that night. Our enthusiasm knew no bounds. Even I, as Bessie Smith sang, who had learned to hold on to a dollar until the eagle grins, went shopping. When we met at the theatre at 6 o'clock all the talk was about, "where do you think we are going?" The clock read 7. And then the clock read 8. Not a single official or secretary had shown. Someone ran to the station. A group went to the hotel where the managers had stayed. The answer was the same. They had all left the night before. Some began to panic as they thought of their financial condition. For the first time I heard about company after company being stranded in Italy. No one had mentioned that before. We all had contracts, but they seemed to be worthless. Some went to the police station. They were indifferent. Someone suggested that I call the American Embassy however, I assured them that "they would not give a dam in those quarters".

When we finally accepted the fact that we had been dumped, we began to go our separate ways. Some one called after me, "Ruth where are you going". I replied, "I'm going to take these crooks to the Lord." The last thing I remember saying out loud that night was, "Lord, you know more about this situation than I do, and you know I need help."

I slept soundly. At ten o'clock the next morning I made a telephone call to the office of the producers of Niagara.

Mr. Mario answered. I said, "Mr Mario, this is Ruth Reese. I am stranded in Firenze, I wonder can you help me."

"Give me the number of the telephone from which you are calling. I did. "Ruth I will call you back in 15 or 20 minutes."

"Thanks", I said, "I will wait." In 20 minutes he called. He had arranged a TV and Radio program. "Come by the office when you arrive in Milano. When I came to the office the next day, not a single word was said about leaving a company of 30 or 40 people stranded in Firenze.

After my Radio and TV show Mario sent me to Madrid to sing at a wedding party for one of the Noble families of Spain whose daughter was getting married. I was booked into the Rupe Tarpeaa a swank Restaurant in Rome. After two weeks there I was moved into the "Jicky" Club, which was the hang-out place for the elite of Europe when they came to Rome. It was common to see ex-King Farouk of Egypt with his retinue of women, films stars Elizabeth Taylor, Eva Gardner, Gregory Peck authors like Tennessee William, Arthur Miller and members from the world Jet Set, as they are called.

After Rupe Tarpeaa and the "Jicky" club the top clubs in Italy opened for me. I went to Milano, Genova, Venesia, Torino. It was inevitable that with all of the publicity I was getting, a movie offer would creep in. My first was as an extra in Quo Vadis. I saw the show over and over and could never find myself. In the second, I was a maid to the star. In the third I was a cross between a maid and a superstitious witch with bulging eyes and open mouth. When I was offered the fourth, I told the man to "get lost." Robeson was right when he had said, "The American presentation of blacks on the screen had had a far reaching influence."

I had grown to know and love Italy. I had added a half dozen or so beautiful old Napoletano Folk songs to my repertoire. I think fondly back to those days when I'd sing "Core 'ngrato' and the stage would be strewn with flowers as the audience yelled, Bravo!

XVI
Denmark

The Black Rose had been getting good coverage in the International artist magazines like ECHO, so I was not too surprised when my agent in Rome received a request from Fritz Ruzicka in Denmark. Fritz remembered me from my stint with the Katherine Dunham Dance Ensemble, and wanted me in his cabaret, Mon Coeur, in Copenhagen. So I arrived in Denmark for the second time. Fritz met me at the station and drove me to his home where his partner, Kate Rosen, waited for us with a delicious danish breakfast. For the second time, I met the danish press. And I opened up in Denmark with a TV show.

I must confess though, that after all of the glitter in Revue and cabaret in Italy, Mon Coeur fell a little flat for me. To hear that clitter-clatter made by people eating and waiters passing up and down in front of me while I tried to "emote" was annoying to say the least. My elaborate costumes were a waste. When I complained to Kate she said, "they pay your salary". I found this to be the general attitude in all of Scandinavia. There were few exceptions. There was no such thing as "Show-Time".

Fritz was a collector of toys. I thought this was rather strange for a man nearly 70 years old. He had a clever way of making a big fuss over a customer who brought him a souvenir from whichever country. So almost every night he had a new toy to show to the public. Another thing that impressed me about that pair was their skill in getting publicity for Mon Cocur and her artists. Sometimes I thought them unscrupulous in their methods. I recall the incident that ended our feeling of "comaradie". It was Christmas week.

Fritz invited me to accompany him and Kate to the "Saxogaard" home for poor children, and sing. When I saw Fritz collect his toys in a shopping bags, I wanted to hug him. What a clever way, I thought, to collect toys for poor children. Of course, the press had been alerted. The cameras went clik-clik as the three of us handed out toys to a group of 25 to 30 smiling happy children as I sang "Git on Board Little Children." When the press left, the children really began to enjoy their toys. Suddenly, Fritz looked at his watch and said, "Ruth, we must collect these." When I realised his meaning, I was speechless with disgust. I excused myself and disappeared. I could not stand to face those poor children after I sung with my heart to them and they had responded with love in their hearts, as I hugged and kissed them saying, "glade Jul". I thought those two were the most heartless people one could meet. Our relationship was never the same. However, they were clever in getting publicity and that publicity paid off.

They arranged T.V. and radio shows for me. For Christmas, I did a grand concert in Townhall. I sang "one-night-stands" in many of the Danish towns.

In 1965, it was through a delegation of Norwegian school teachers to a meeting of fellow teachers in Copenhagen, that brought my program, "Negro Music History from 1619 to the Present Time" to the attention of the school authorities in Denmark. For more than two years, I had been touring with this program in Norway under the regime of State Theatre that was lead at that time by Fritz von der Lippe. When the Danish School Division sent me the tour list in 1965, it was for 44 concerts in Gymnasiums and High School. At the end I was told that I could come back every two years with the same program. In the Commercial High School the leaders said that I could repeat every year. And so I was in the Danish schools regularly.

I toured the Friends of Music in Denmark with the program, "Handel's Messiah and 8 Negro Spirituals", comparing the text in each. In this program Handel Messiah and Negro Spirituals, I wanted to hear a part of the Overture from Handel's Messiah. Most of the organists insisted on playing Bach. I changed this program to "The Life Of Christ in Negro Spirituals," I still go occasionally to Denmark with this program.

I have done several tours in Denmark under Gosta Schwarck's management of "Pride of Black Dreams". It has been a success with both public and critics, but somehow I felt that "Pride" was never set up right. It should be in the theatre and not in the concert hall.

XVII
And So Till Norway

Although I knew little of Norway before leaving America, I was not completely ignorant. I had seen a number of Sonja Henie's movies. I know now that these scenes were probably taken in Colorado, but at the time I saw them, we were led to believe that we were seeing Norway. I had heard the story of the "Laplanders" only to discover upon arriving in North Norway in 1958 that the word, "Lapp" was as obnoxious to the Samisk Folk as the word, "nigger" among blacks in the U.S.A.

However, what I had heard about mostly, was skiers. "Norwegian babies are born with skis attached." As King Olav said to me later: "Norwegian children learn to ski before they can talk." When I had taken the night train to Copenhagen headed for my first visit to Norway, friends seeing me off had warned: "Be careful when you go on skis that you break an arm or leg and not your neck. At least you will be able to sing." When the train reached Halden, I was up with my eyes pinned to the landscape. Everytime the train passed a hill, I expected to see people racing down on skis. After nearly two hours when the train crawled into the Oslo station, I had not seen a single person on skis.

It was crisp, sparkling Monday morning in mid-November 1956. The taxi-man took about two minutes in his drive to Hotel Astoria. When I offered him a choice of Danish or Swedish money, he chose Swedish. As usually, I was anxious and a little nervous coming to a new place and a strange country. At the reception desk, a young man speaking perfect English, welcomed me to Norway for the first time. Upon giving me the keys to my room, he stated that the director would talk to me at breakfast. He directed one of the piccolos to help carry my baggage to room 436. I was very pleased when I saw the room. It was in the back part of the house, I knew it would be quiet. I had been given a room with toilet and bath and a marvellous reading lamp beside the bed. I was not aware then, but I was to enjoy that room many times. Everytime I came to Astoria, I was given my room, 436. After freshening up a bit, I went down to the restaurant to partake of my first Norwegian "Breakfast". It was a cosy, intimate place. I fell in love with it at once.

After a while, a rather small woman came over to my table, introduced herself and bade me wlecome. When I tried to talk to her about repertoire, she stated that the pianist, and the Hammond organ expert would talk of that. Her manner had been so brisk, I was unnerved for a minute. I could not for the life of me think of anything of which to talk. Kate and Fritz had been very dubious about my coming to Astoria. When I had asked Kate details of the contract, she had stated that my contract would come from Astoria. "Just send us the usual ten per cent." I knew something was wrong. Kate and Fritz did not do business in that way. So, as soon as I could, I mentioned Kate to Miss Rokke.

Miss Rokke was even more bristle in manner and fairly boomed: "Your being here has nothing to do with that woman and I will have absolutely no traffic with either she or her man." I was afraid to comment further. I surely did not wish to get off on the wrong foot before I started. After a while Miss Rokke left me to finish my breakfast alone. I was very glad.

Promptly at 11 o'clock both pianist and organist came. They were both friendly but shy. We talked first about the public and repertoire. They would leave a choice of songs to me. Good. However, to my chagrin, I found that I was expected to do three shows each night, something I had never done in all of Europe. But it was also something I knew should have been discussed before I found myself sitting in Astoria talking to the pianist. That was my blunder. I soon found out that Miss Rokke simply wanted continuous entertainment while her guests ate their dinner. Her knowledge of Cabaret was unquestionable nil. Yet she had a locale that could have been a top entertainment spot on a world level. Astoria Lille Cabaret was cosy, intimate with a tasteful decor. I am almost certain Miss Rokke never saw that side of her restaurant.

After two days, my engagement was extended for two weeks, a very good sign. At the end of the month, I was offered a 6 month contract for the coming season. Because of commitments in Sweden and Denmark, I had to refuse. I accepted a month.

When I came back to Astoria for the third time, I felt more secure. I knew Miss Rokke liked my work although she had never said so. The fact that she had wanted me back for the 6 month period spoke reams. Also, I had a feeling that she liked me as a person. For three Sundays she had invited me to spend the day with she and her family on her country farm. We carried left overs from the restaurant and gave them to her pigs and chickens. I got a chance to see her minks. I enjoyed plucking up eggs to take back to Astoria.

I had a new pianist who was a little more flexible and much more open to modern ideas. I decided to be smart. I thought that because Miss Rokke liked me as an artist and as a person, I could "pull the wool over her eyes". I would play the fox to her brother rabbit. My pianist and I decided to put a little international flavour into our act. The restaurant had steps inside leading to the second floor. But they were never used. The public entered the restaurant from the street. We resolved that for

the first time in Astoria's history, we would use
these steps in our act.

In Italy a seamstress had created a fabulous gown
for me in a cream-coloured satin cloth embroidered
with jewels and sequinns with a train almost 2
metres long. I would make a grand entrance for the
first show only. It was 9 o'clock on the dot. The
restaurant was packed. My picture had been in all
of the Oslo papers. Guests had overflowed to the
small side rooms. The pianist made a fan-fare on
the piano and the organist echoed it on his
Hammond. With his right hand raised, the pianist
intoned: Ladies and Gentlemen from Paris, France,
the Black Rose. I floated slowly down the steps
looking every bit like the Hollywood version of the
Queen of Sheba. The reception was electric. People
stopped eating with their forks midway between
their plates and their mouth. Waiters bringing in
food on trays halted in their tracks. The applause
was deafening. Without any further introduction,
I began to sing, Bixio's "Lasciami Cantata Una
Conzone Con Te". For fifteen minutes, they listened
to me sing. I was bursting with pride.

Before I went to my room, I arranged to meet
the musicians at 11 o'clock the next day. We would
discuss how we could make the show even better.
We would give Oslo a real Cabaret.

When we met at 11 o'clock, I noticed at once
that Per Brunn-Lie, the pianist, looked crest-fallen.
Frank Hanson, the organist, avoided looking at me,

for I was smiling from ear to ear. I burst out at once: "How did she like it?" "Ruth", Per said sadly, "She told us to tell you to forget about the coming down the steps, just get on with the singing." I knew that Miss Rokke had seen the same scene that I had recorded when I entered in all my regalia the night before. People had stopped eating and their eating was her business. She would have nothing that she thought would distract them.

I had a feeling that Per and Frank were waiting for the explosion of my artistic temper but I happen to be one artist who uses artistic temperament only on the stage, hardly ever off stage. We sat silently for a while, shook our heads and then I said: "And so we just get on with the singing, huh?" Miss Rokke acted as if nothing had happened. The next Sunday, we were back at her mink farm feeding the pigs and chickens and plucking eggs.

On the last day, when I went to the office for my pay, I was informed by the secretary that Miss Rokke wanted me back for Spring season. Like Frank, I was beginning to feel like an institution. Once I had asked Frank how long he had been at Astoria and he had said: "Oh me, I just go on and on. I have been here for years." I was beginning to feel the same. And then fate stepped in and frustrated all of the plans I had made for myself.

On my last night for that period, I met an absolutely crazy man. He was a friend of Per Bruunie's. Per had met him in the street that day and had

asked him: "Why haven't you been to Astoria to
hear our Black Bird sing?" And so, he had come.
Per presented him to me before the Show started:
"This is Bookhandler, Paul Shetelig". My mind was
on my coming performance so I was not particularly
impressed. To me, he was just another guest in the
restaurant. I said the usual, "I hope you enjoy the
Show" and continued on my way. When I came in
to sing, I noticed that he sat alone at a small table
right in front of the stage. I also noted that his
applause was quite sparse when I sang Gershwin,
Cole Porter and my Neopolitana Folk Songs.
However, when I sang the second Show which
included songs like Fats Waller's "Aint MisBehavin
and Handy's St Louise Blues," I thought he would
never stop clapping his hands. Afterwards, I
received an invitation from him to have dinner, but
I had already accepted an invite from friends who
heard me sing "Lasciami Cantare Una Conzone
Con Te", a song they liked very much. Always
when I work in Cabaret, I leave as fast as possible
because of the smoke. As usually, the headwaiter
had prepared me a tray of "supper" which I always
took to my room.

When I rose to leave this Paul Shetelig came over
to me with a polite bow and said: "May I carry
your tray for you?" We took the elevator up to my
room. At the door, he handed me the tray and with
another bow said. "A thousand thanks for St. Louis
Blues, I have never heard it sung better. I would

like to see you again, what about tomorrow?" "I am sorry," I said, "I have planned to leave tomorrow!"

Early the next morning the room maid knocked at my door bringing a package that had been left for me at the desk. Upon opening it, I found Neville Shute's "No Highway" with the following words inscribed: "Dear Ruth, it is impossible to buy flowers on Sundays in this silly town and I therefore hope you will enjoy this book. I have to thank you for the wonderful way in which you interpreted the good old St Louis Blues. It made a big impression on me. And so did your big lovely eyes and that wonderful smile of yours. I hope to be seeing you again soon. Best wishes from, Paul." That did it.

For the first time in Europe, I had met a man who was appealing to my brain before trying to get into my bed. I had to be in Gavle on Thursday so I decided to stay in Oslo another two days. Around 12 o'clock, I had a telephone call: "I would like your permission to show you a little around Oslo." During the periods I had been to Oslo, I had a few friends who insisted on taking me to Theatre Cafe where we usually met a number of half-drunk, boring people talking a lot of nonsense, while I would rather have remained in my hotel room with a good book.

It was beautiful weather in Oslo. We walked down to the wharf and took a boat over to Bygdoy. We walked slowly through the autumn-coloured trees to the Folk Museum and then to the Viking

Ships. Paul proved to be a fantastic guide. I understood at once that he was enthusiastic over Norwegian history and geography. That evening, he took me to Chat-Noir, where I saw some of my colleagues from Astoria perform. After the Show, he saw me to Astoria, kissed my hand and said: "Thanks for today, I will see you tomorrow."

The next day, we went to the National Gallery and to Vigeland Museum. We had lunch and then we took the train to Holmenkollen Ski Jump. From there we walked slowly back to town while he talked and talked. I understood very soon that The man loved to walk and talk. I suppose it was natural for him to ask about my future plans. We parted on the Wednesday with a promise to keep in touch. Upon arriving in my room in Central Hotel in Gavle, Sweden, the first thing I noticed on the small table was a bowl of fruit and a single rose.

"Well, what do you know, how nice," I said out loud to myself. A half-hour later there came a "telephone for you from Oslo, Norway". Thus he had set a pattern that he has followed for more than 20 years. In addition to the fruit on March 10th, there would be added a half bottle of Veuve Clicquot Sec Champagne. On opening nights, wherever I was in Europe there was that bowl of fruit, the little rose and best wishes, from Paul. What woman could resist. I decided I would live in Norway. I had been travelling around Europe for more than 7 years without a fixed address. I had left packages in several places. Now I would assemble them in Oslo. From Copenhagen came a large trunk of costumes I had not seen for two years. From Paris came costumes I had not seen for years, cartons of music and personal things I had forgotten I owned. One precious item I have not retrieved was the box containing books and family photos. So Christmas was at hand.

Paul and I wanted to be together. Of all the places in Europe, Paul concluded that we should spend our first Christmas together in a town called, Drobak. However, Drobak proved to be a charming place and it is amusing to think that it was exactly 26 years ago in quaint little Drobak, that I decided to be a norwegian. During the Christmas week, we explored every corner of Drobak. In concession to my old-fashioned up-bringing, Paul took me to little Drobak Church. Little did we think then, that 26 years later during the Drobak Cultural Week that I would stand in that church and sing a Gospel Concert accompanied by the Magnolia Jazz Band to a standing-room-only crowd.

Even though I saw what was coming, it was impossible for me to turn back. It was in 1960 that Paul and I decided that Norway would be home. Paul had been divorced for some 6 years when I met him. When it became obvious to his friends that we were serious, they suddenly became interested in his welfare. But we both knew that real friends would wish us luck even though they thought we were being stupid for after all it was a private matter between two grown-up people. But some of the comments and reactions were comical and we enjoyed exchanging our experiences at dinner.

One of Paul's friends had said to him one day: "Paul you are betraying norwegian womanhood, it is alright for you to go to bed with Ruth, we can understand that. But don't even entertain the thought of marrying her." One evening we sat in Bristol Restaurant when a man Paul had thought of as his "best" friend, came over to our table. Naturally Paul invited him to sit. After a short time this "Best" friend, with a broad smile on his face turned to me and said, "Ruth, you must excuse me for saying this, but you know I sorta like these blue-eyed blonds," he said as he waved his hand in the air. With a broader smile on my face, I answered: "Yes, as Mrs O'Leary said, every man to his own liking, as she kissed the cow." He shot a quick, puzzled glance at Paul, but at that time Paul was as ignorant as he about the stories of Mrs O'Leary who was milking the cow that kicked over the lamp that started the great Chicago fire. But he shut up. We weathered the storm.

XVIII
Home

I had visited Chat Noir Theatre only once before during one of my "passing through periods". We were enjoying the show immensely. At the high point of the Show, there came on one of the most depressing sights a black person can witness. Five grotesque, black faced, thick lipped, spitting and singing clowns entered the stage. It was suppose to be a parody on the Deep River Boys, who were quite popular in Norway at the time. My first impulse was to leave, but I was not quite sure if Paul would understand such a demonstration. Up to that time I had not discussed my mode of protesting such scenes. So we stayed to the end of the Show. Now a year later or so, I am on my way for a second visit. Paul hoped, "there won't be any unpleasant incidents this time."

The programme started out fine. I was very happy to see some of the artists with whom I had worked in Astoria Cabaret. And then it happened. To close the second Act, in crept a well known singer. One would not have known who it was if the name had not been on the program. She had a protruding

stomach, over stuffed breasts and acted like an
abnormal heavy set vulgar wash-woman in her run-
down heels and shabby clothes. She came on
singing some nonsense song about a norwegian
"stinker" called Larsen. This was supposed to be a
parody on Ella Fitzgerald's relation with this
Larsen. Now, I will admit that Ella, like many of
the rest of us, have gotten a little thick in spots over
the years. Nevertheless, Ella is an elegant artists
when she walks out on any stage to sing. Famous
artists can always risk being imitated. However,
this parody went too far. It took on a racial slur
and it attacked her private life.

It was impossible for me to see this act and not
re-act. I was a member of the "Committee for the
Negro in the Arts" whose sole aim was to fight just
such stereotypes that I had witnessed on my first
and second visit to Chat Noir. I remembered
Canada Lee's and Paul Robeson's counsel, "wherever you meet stereotypes, do something about it."

I wrote an article and took it to Aftenposten, they
took it. However, what they did with it was indeed
rare. Instead of printing it as I had written, they
took out certain extracts. In the end my criticism
read as an interview. I called it very bad press
behaviour.

Quite often, during this same period, I saw a
group on T.V., who came out dressed in Al Jolson's
revolting type of minstral make-up. Everytime I
saw them on T.V., I wrote my complaint to the

Entertainment Department. No response. Weeks later the same group held forth. Several times norwegian TV has shown a program of a group of white singers from BBC in black face, thick-lipped Al Jolson make-up. They did not sing a single black song. Why the make-up? Why do some people think it is funny to see white singers and actors painted as blacks, when what they are doing has absolutely nothing to do with any black art form? If BBC really wanted to make a program of black music, there are a number of talented blacks living in London.

I wrote some lines of criticism. One of the readers wrote a "brilliant" reply that I would like to share with you. He headlined it, "Here is the answer to the problem, Ruth Reese". "You are a sore head. You are an enemy of the Negro People. What do you think of a parody on Orientals. Why do Nigerians discriminate against other Nigerians. Why don't you criticize the black reclaim on the outside of the box that contains "Black Man's Cigars? I thought the Show was great". The poor reader did not mention a single point that I had tried to make in my article.

I guess I am pretty naive. I could not understand why producers ignored my criticism of their showing these "stereotypes" on TV. They continuted for a long time after I had written my first charge. Even in the 1980s, I occasionally spot an Al Jolson "black" among their studio listeners when they are required to come in Carnival dress. Usually, I refuse all invitations to participate in Carnivals because of this fact.

It did not take me long to understand that I would face the same problems here as in America. I was a black in a white society. Nevertheless, I had made my choice. Norway would be home. I wanted no special favours. I knew the norwegians, generally, as all other people the world over, would accept me. My trouble would come from the small group in control where bigotry is carried out behind closed doors, "Board Members". I knew I would have to struggle. However, I would do as Aunt Bella had advised, "I would put on the whole armour and be ready for the battle." I would work to make my programs good.

XIX
Race Hate and Democracy

In 1959 newspapers all over the world were full of the story of Little Rock, Arkansas, where nine black students had been admitted to Central High School. Their treatment inside of the school by teachers, principal and students was as cruel as the mob outside waiting for them each morning and afternoon. All over the south, black Churches were being bombed. Black leaders were being kidnapped and murdered. Why are they attacking the churches, I was asked. I decided to lecture about it. I would call it, "Race Hate in a Democracy". On January 20, 1960, I was on the Speakers podium in the University Aula.

To my great surprise, the hall was almost full. The American Cultural Attache and his retinue sat on the first two rows. Up to that time, everytime I had had a concert in Oslo I had sent them free tickets. Up to this day, I have not received a word of thanks or acknowledgement. However, for my lecture in the Aula, I had purposefully ommitted sending them an invitation. But here they were, out in full force, to hear what I had to say about their country.

At that time I was constantly receiving reports of surveys made by accredited organisations in America. I was especially sure of the facts I would present. I ended the lecture with my version of Lewis Allen's "Strange Fruit". The first person to congratulate me after the lecture was the American Cultural Attache. How naive I was. He remarked on how well documented it was and wanted to know my source of information. I gave it to him. I had been using that source of information for two years. After that night, I have never had a line from them again. I have written. Not a word in reply. A very lively debate followed in the Norwegian papers. Every paper in Oslo carried a report of my lecture. At first the readers were addressing me. And then they started lecturing each other.

I toured with "Race Hate in a Democracy" in the 14 County for Folk Academies and other organisations. In every place, newspapers covered each lecture and debates followed. I suppose it was natural that I would be personally attacked in the news. I began to read, "Ruth Reese, go home", "Ruth Reese, we love Louis Armstrong because he sticks to his singing."

One American student said to me, "do you realise that you are giving Russia "fodder" for her propaganda mill?" He did not seem to understand that the USA was furnishing, by her lack of action against those who were bombing black churches and her blatant mistreatment of her black citizens, the Soviet Union all the "fodder" needed for her propaganda. I began to encounter many Americans like him. They are not so concerned about how badly blacks are treated in the USA. Their worry is that other people will get to know about it.

Later I was sitting in the lobby of the Atlantic Hotel in Stavanger after a lecture. I was reading some comments about my lecture. I was feeling a little dejected when the voice of the Secretary of the United Nations, lifted my spirits with the remark, "I have been reading about you. You are absolutely right. Keep it up, and good luck." It is true some blacks have reached the top rung in America but too often it has been at the expense of his integrity and by betraying his brother. Sometimes I challenge blacks in the diplomatic service of the USA. "Diplomats," I read somewhere once, "Are the best citizens of their respective lands, who are chosen to tell lies for their country". I met a brother in Park Hotel in Goteberg. He invited me to dinner. I asked him, "what answers are you giving people around the world when they ask about the treatment of people of colour in the USA."

"Well, sister, I try to make them believe that America is doing 90 per cent when I know that she is only doing less than 10, but what the hell, on my own I could never make a trip like the one I have made. I have lived like a King in the best hotels,

ate the finest food available. I travel first class. I
get chauffeured car wherever I go. Now I am
inviting you to have dinner. Order what you will,
the State Department is paying for it."

"Are you sure of that," I asked. He assured me
he was, "Whatever your heart desires, order it."
He laughed heartily as I said, "For a starter, I
would like Russian Caviar with a glass of Veuve
Cliquot Sec Champagne." He nearly cracked up as
he said. "You are my sister". He hailed the waiter
and placed my order.

XX
Building a New Repertoire

I must admit that in the back of my mind when I was planning coming to Europe, was the idea that some years here would enhance my chances to make money in the USA. After only a few years, I had changed my mind. I thought I knew America. However, I had not realised the depth of the wound inflicted on my people. As Lawrence Brown had said to me: "Just wait until you are over there for a time and look back. You will really see your country for the first time." I am sure that few blacks in America realise the extent to which they have been deprived. They took even our names from us. And they have tried and are still striving to nudge us out of history. It was these thoughts that gave impetus to my future plan as an artist in Norway.

More than one manager in places where I have followed the great Josephine Baker and others, have said to me: "Ruth, Miss Baker has nothing on you." And when I reminded them of the differences in salary, to a man they have said: "Yes, it is unfair. Why don't you go back to the States for a year or so and then come back under management." I knew what they meant. Go to the States, hire an agent, give him whatever percentage of my salary he required. The agent would then proceed with an "image-build up" campaign of me, later send me back to Europe, billed as a "Super" and the public would pay a high price, would not dare criticise. The idea revolted me. I saw now my mission clearly.

I would organise a series of programmes based upon Negro Culture and Folklore, using the different music forms in a Historic perspective. I knew there was no money in it.

The American Negro Music History from 1619 to the Present Time was the first of my new programs. It began with an African Lullaby followed by an african war chant, Sorrow Spirituals, Protest Spirituals, Church Spirituals, Worksongs, Negro Lullaby, Blues, Jazz, Ragtime, Plantation songs and Gospels. The program also included songs showing the influence of Negro Music on American white composers. I closed this program with Lewis Allan's "Strange Fruit". The leader of the State Concert Theatre engaged me at once for tours in Gymanasiums, Teachers Schools and Folk Academies. Through the norwegian teacher schools, the news of my program came to Denmark and Sweden and East Germany.

The three programs were produced for television and I will for once be modest and say it was "one of the best ever produced in Norwegian T.V." I'm only quoting the critics.

The Life of Christ in Negro Spirituals grew out of an idea I had of comparing the text of Handel's messiah with the text of Negro Spirituals. I had been hearing Handel's Messiah performed in my church every Christmas and Easter since I was a child. Suddenly the idea struck me, build a program on the idea. I chose 8 arias from Handel and 8 Negro Spirituals with the same motive. I divided the program into four parts: Jesus comes to earth, His life on earth, His crucifixion and resurrection and Christianity triumphs on earth. Although this program went very well in Denmark, I found church organists a little cold to Handel's music. And in Norway, I found the idea of Handel's music and Negro Spirituals coupled together, was not too popular. So I substituted the 8 arias from Handel with 8 spirituals and called the program. "The life of Christ in Negro Spirituals."

PRIDE OF BLACK DREAMS

the most dramatic of my programs is the summary of the Afro-american struggle from 1619 to the present day. It was done in song and recitation. Other programs builded during this period were:

Lyrical Poetry of American Black Poets
Black Women Stood up and Fought
We Shall Overcome
Cabaret Nostalgi

The real Gospel Songs
Segregation in South Africa
Freedom for Namibia.

I recognised at once that with these programs, I
could become a unique artist. I was not only intro-
ducing new material, I was presenting a new style
of concert, The Kaseri or Lecture Concert. I was
stamped by both public and critics, "Ruth Reese
and her special way . . . " I was so happy. I cried
my thanks to God. I had wanted to get away from
the stereotype way of giving concerts. I had wanted
to place my folk music on par with the best European music. The fact that I had finally found what
I like to think of as my "niche" in Norway's Music
Life, did not mean that my troubles were over. The
first program was swimming along smoothly until
State Concert Bureau was established. State
Theatre Bureau had agreed not to engage singers
any longer. I went over to State Concert Bureau. I
was accepted. For that I shall always be grateful.
Under State Theatre Bureau's regime, I had
performed for an adult public. Under State Concert
Bureau, I was sent into the Junior High School.

I have often wonder why, with all of the information I could give of Negro Folklore and Culture,
they insisted on sending me to entertain children.
For I had to rearrange my whole approach to my
program. And I must say, I amused them well. All
over, I heard School leaders say and some of them

wrote to State Concert Bureau "thats the best program State Concert Bureau has sent us." Now I find people in my audience who heard me 20 years ago sing that program declare that "your concert was the high point of my school days." However, what I am trying to say is this. At this time there was an increased interest all over Norway for Negro Music. Almost every month, I received letters from teachers and students wanting to know about the different music forms in Negro music. This was exactly what my program, "The American Negro Music History from 1619 to the Present Time" was about.

Why would State Concert Bureau send out a graduate of Northwestern University School of Music to norwegian children instead of to the Gymnasiums and Teachers Schools where the need was greater. At least student teachers would have understood and could have made use of the material which I could have given. It forces me to conclude that that is the fate of the black immigrant in a white society. It is difficult to overlook the colour and see the value of the individual.

"The Real Gospel Songs" were late in coming to Europe. I have always felt it a pity that Europeans heard the commercial side of Gospel Music before they heard of Thomas A Dorsey, the founder of Gospel. Dorsey created the style and gave it the name "Gospel" in the early 1920s. To try to rectify this I organised a program which I have called,

"The Real Gospel Songs" in order to distinguish it
from the many varieties of programs one can read
and hear being stamped, "Gospel". I was lucky in
finding the pianist who understands what I mean
by a "gospel beat" in contrast to a "jazz beat".

PRIDE OF BLACK DREAMS is really my best
program, at least its the most elaborate, 6 costumed
acts. Director Anker Edding, who had given me my
first North Norway tour in 1958, was now director
in Tonsberg. When I wrote and told him I had an
idea for a "One Woman Show", he had answered:
"Welcome to Klubben". We premiered it in
October 1969. It was a Success! Really, I had not
read such flowery critics since leaving Italy. I was
declared a "fully-fledged" first class entertainer
again.

XXI
And Speaking of Colour

One of Norway's music critics and I sat in the dressing room in the Universitet Aula waiting for my appearance with the City Symphony Orchestra in a School Concert. He had just heard the day before a program on the radio that I had made of Black Opera Singers. Some weeks preceding, I had read Hans Jorgen Hurum's full page article in the Aftonposten on Opera Singers. He had not mentioned a single black. Hence my program. I went to the radio archives and made two programs on Black Opera Singers and the difficulty they were having trying to break through the racial bars of Opera, especially in the USA. Our conversation led to Felicia Weathers who was engaged to sing, I think it was Traviata with the norwegian opera in a few days.

He agreed with me that her voice is magnificent. However, he said, "I just don't like to see black singers in such roles and I guess Ruth, you would call that discrimination." "Yes", I said, "I would call that downright prejudice on your part". Then I asked him, "how can you accept a norwegian in the role of "Madam Butterfly?" He said only, "Oooom" and I continued, "Why don't you just close your eyes at the beginning of the Opera, when there is a black singer. Listen only to the voice. Get involved in the story. You will be surprised. You will forget the colour of the singer's skin." "Alright" he said, "I will try."

I waited anxiously for his criticism the next day. How naive of me. If the perpetrators, fosters and nourishers of discrimination openly declared themselves, how much easier it would be to attack and defeat them. No. He acquiesced in the storming applause the public gave Felicia. Or maybe, he took my advice and closed his eyes. Anyway, I like to think that he did. It is interesting to note that although the number of Black Opera Singers have multiplied in the last years, few, if any guests the norwegian opera. And yet, one would be shocked to know how many foreigners there are in the norwegian opera, all white, of course.

As I said, the walls of prejudice has many shields. I questioned a producer in the theatre about an artist I knew who had much experience in acting. I wanted to know why this person was not used. He replied that the language was faulty, "some of the words", he said, "are not enunciated properly or there is something wrong in the inflection etc." I reminded him that these things could be learned along with lines. And then I said, "now, with all the different dialects found in Norway, what difference

would one more make?" One of the first things
noticeable to strangers upon coming to Norway is
that every citizen speaks his own language.

An incident comes to mind from the first visit I
made to Norway. I saw a show in Chat Noir. I was
presented to the director. I was making quite a hit
in Italy after my success in Niagra Follies, the
cabaret Rupy Tarpee and Jicky Club in Rome.
Entertaining music was a natural for me. I
mentioned these events to the director. He answered
that in a "week or two I shall be going to Paris to
look around, if I see a coloured part, I shall
remember you."

Writing about this now brings to mind a story
Conrad told me. He auditioned for the Ballet in the
opera. They told him that he was a beautiful
dancer, but that his presence on stage might disturb
the eyes of the public. Just one more colour story.

One of the theatres announced the coming
production of an "all coloured play". There would
be some 30 actors on stage. Most of them in crowd
scenes. "Ah, ha", I said to myself, "here is my
chance." I did not even think of speaking a line.
Paul and I were in the theatre soon after this
announcement. During intermission, we met the
producer in the lobby. I said to him, "At last, I am
sure that this play will have a part for me, when
shall I report for rehearsal?" A couple of years
before this, one of my strapping, husky black african
friends had been offered the part of a slave in one

of the theatre productions. He is nearly two metres high, just the type a plantation owner would enjoy "breaking". My friend, instead of being grateful for the offer, created quite a sensation because he threatened to "cuff" the producer for trying to insult him.

However, there would be no slaves in the coming production. The populace would consist of ordinary black people. The producer of the future Drama looked at my husband and said in all seriousness: "Paul, you know we could never have a real Negro on the stage with the rest." I smiled to myself as I thought of all the varied colours of coloured people. Paul, equally as serious as the producer said, "Yes, I understand." Before I could ask him what it was he understood, the bell rang for us to go back to our seats in the theatre.

It is now 1984. I am in the midst of celebrating my 25 or more years in Norwegian music life. There have been unbelievable changes. Would you believe that in March of this year, I had a concert in lillesand where my accompaniment was a Violin Orchestra, trained by Ivar Skippervold, of 23 children between the ages of 7 and 13 years old. And when I think of North Norway in 1958 and what it was like even in the 1970s, 15 years later the changes are unbelievable.

XXII
And Finally

I have asked myself many times, "if I could do it all over again, what would I change?" I would alter very little. I would have kept on the International Circuit longer. When I chose to make norway my permanent home, I gradually confined my performances to Scandinavia. Only once in a while, I ventured back into wider Europe. And of course, I always give concerts in the USA, especially in Chicago and Alabama, when I am there on a visit. But to maintain a home, I felt that I should be in it. I have read over and over through the years, interviews of famous artists who say that they are home only one or two months in the year. I could grasp this if the two were in the same profession and travelling together.

When I decided to make singing a career, I haunted the concert halls in Chicago. In the 1940s, we could point to only four people of colour whom top white management had given the stamp of approval in classic music, Paul Robeson, Marian Anderson, Dorothy Mayner and Roland Hayes. Of course, we knew this to be false. There were hundreds of black singers in the USA who were just as good as the above named four, but the power of projection lay with white management who owned the business. Even some blacks accepted this judgment without any questions.

I was 15 or 16 years old when I heard Marian Anderson for the first time. Sol Hurok of the Colombia Concert Agency had just taken her over. Coming out of Orchestra Hall, a woman from my community who knew that I was studying to become a singer stopped me on the steps and asked: "well, young lady, how did you like the great Marian Anderson?" I was naive enough to think that she honestly wanted my frank opinion so I said: "I don't see how a singer can expect to make contact with her public with her eyes closed." I had noticed that almost everytime Anderson began a song, she closed her eyes and usually kept them closed until the song was finished. I later read in an interview her saying that she closed her eyes because the audience disturbed her. And then I continued: "And she ought to hire a dress maker, she looks awful."

The woman, who had asked for my impression turned to her friends and said in derision: "Well, well, well, look who has the nerve to criticise Marian Anderson." She and her friends laughed as they walked away. From that moment, I learned to keep my ideas, specially of singers, to myself unless my views were in accord with the conception of the one who asked my judgement. However it was interesting to read the critics in the Chicago Tribune the next day. Claudia Cassidy, the Pauline Hall of Chicago, but with a little more acid, had hit upon the same two points I had mentioned. At first, I had thought to send the clippings to the woman who had tried to insult me. After thinking it over, I decided it was not worth the stamp because the lady had totally mis-understood me and her estimation of me was certainly not important to my advancement.

While the above named black singers were being hailed as "special", black instrumentalists, composers and conductors were finding it next to impossible to get a hearing. We all know the story of Scott Joplin and his Opera, Treemonisha. In 1935, Ray Nance, who later became famous with Duke Ellington's orchestra, created a sensational music wave in a classic concert in Orchestra Hall. He was hailed by critics as a black Nicole Paganini because of violin tone quality and fingering. However, agents stated that the American public was not ready to accept black musicians in classical music. Eddie South, another brilliant violinist had knocked in vain at the same door. The story of pianist Teddy Wilson and many others, is well known.

By 1940, my mind was fixed on being a singer. I became a dedicated concert-goer, not only to concerts by black artist but to whites as well. I had to travel to the loop which was about an hours ride

by bus from my home on the southside to hear
what was referred to as "arrived" artists. With the
possible exception of Paul Robeson and Roland
Hayes, they were all, black and white, singing the
same type of program. In a Robeson program, one
heard a variety of Folk Songs from many lands
in their original language. From Roland Hayes, I
learned that Negro Spirituals could be sheer joy.
The usual program consisted of Old English and
Italian, German Lieder, a couple of Arias, Intermission. After a 15 minute interval the artist came
back with a group of modern English and if the
artist was black one heard a group of Negro Spirituals. And here again except for Roland Hayes,
singers "wobbled" around in the classics when they
sang Spirituals. They tried to leave out the "blue
notes" that characterises black music. I never heard
a white singer do a black composition and for them
to try to sing a Spiritual, was unheard of. Even
some black singers refused to sing them.

In Oslo I remember hearing a well-known black
singer answer in a very annoyed manner an inter-
viewer who asked her why she did not include
Negro Spirituals in her program: "Negro Spirituals
are not a part of my background and I don't know
anything about them." "Poor thing", I commented
to Paul as I heard her say that.

What I was hearing in the USA in the 1940s
were artists billed as Americas best. They were all
extending European music. Voices could be

wonderful. However, I found the same material quite boring after a time. I was not satisfied with what I was hearing. Unconsciously, I think, it was my early appreciation of the value of my peoples music that underlined my desire to raise it to the level of recognition of the music I was hearing at these concerts each week. I pledged to dedicate my musical life to this cause. Black Composers of classical music in the European style like Florence Price and Margaret Bonds, who were on a par with the best European creators of classical music, were heard only in our community. I know it is dangerous to break with tradition, still I was determined to do so. Cautiously I began.

I tried what I thought was a totally new idea in 1961 in my Wigmore Hall Concert in London. First I sang a group of Negro Spirituals, a group of Negro Folk Songs. After intermission, I sang two arias, a group of Old English and ended the concert with a group of Brahms. I was in the middle of my second Spiritual, "Git on Board, Little Children", when I became conscious that the black, white-haired man sitting on the front bench was my old teacher and friend, Lawrence Brown who had written, "Git On Board". On impulse, I waved and he waved back. From that moment, I was doubly inspired. We had a marvellous reunion back stage after the concert. The first thing Brown wanted to know, was "where did you get the idea of singing Spirituals first on your programme." And then he told me a fantastic story.

In the 1920s he had travelled over Europe on tour with Roland Hayes, our great tenor. Hayes had arranged Spirituals for the first half of his program and German Leider, for which he had a perfect diction, for the second half. They noticed that as they began the second group, the audience became restless and talkative and some even left the hall. They were giving a concert in Dresden, Germany. The public, as usual was enthusiastic over the first half. As Hayes began his group of Schubert some of the public actually hissed. Hayes stopped in the middle of a song and whispered something to Brown. Brown began to play a new number "Du Bist Die Ruh". It worked like magic. Brown said that when Hayes reached the end of that number, one could hear the proverbial "pin drop in a haystack". "It was really eerie", Brown said. And then the hissers stood up and applauded. They had no more trouble after that. Nevertheless, to be on the safe side, Hayes placed his Spirituals last on the program. And like sheep, other singers had done the same. Brown said that I was the first one he had heard of to change that custom.

Also in 1961, my opportunity to try my idea of a blended programme; of European classics, Negro Spirituals, Blues and Jazz Evergreens to a packed house in Bergen was a good idea. If the classic critics were present, they gave no evidence of the fact.

During this period of my career, I was terribly disturbed and the presentation of a Medal to me by the Norweigan Student Society in 1963, frustrated me even more. It was during the height of the Civil Rights movement in the USA. I wanted to be there. I wanted to be a part of that fight. In fact, I was beginning to feel guilty as I read about persons whom I knew being jailed, beaten and sometimes killed in the struggle while I sat safe in Oslo. Again I found a clue of what I could do in the remarks made by the chairman when my Medal was being penned. He had said: "To Ruth Reese for her contribution of information that has increased our understanding of the black problem in America."

I remembered the promise I had made to myself and to Paul Robeson in 1950. Robeson never tired of discussing how an artist could serve the people with his art. In answer to my question of how he could give up such a lucrative career, he replied, "I did it for you and for all the other blacks who will come after you." And with fervour I had said, "thanks, I will never forget." I have never forgotten. Dr. Martin Luther King's advice to me upon meeting him in 1964 was: "It is good to have people like you who can truthfully interpret our movement in Europe, keep it up". As I lay in bed the same night, I thought to myself, this is the fight I have

been in all of my life. I remembered the incident of
the "flag" when I was barely 13 years old. I thought
of our family struggle with charity workers.
However, I thought that now I am equipped to do
something concrete.

I had proven that I could, if I kept in mind
style and tradition, sing all forms of music. I had
demonstrated that I could be a writer of sorts. I
had been travelling in Europe for only a short time
when I discovered that little was known of Black
people other than boxers, athletes and Jazz
musicians. Whenever I mentioned black scholars
like W.E.B. DuBois or Carter G. Woodson, the
Historian, freedom fighters like Harriet Tubman
and Frederick Douglass and the creator of the Blood
Bank idea, Dr Charles Drew and a long list of
Inventors, I was hardly believed. I was travelling
in England in 1951 when the idea of writing about
these individuals came to me. Whenever I found
myself in Paris, Rome and London, I spent my
spare time researching in the Libraries for material
on Negro history. By the time I reached Oslo in
1956, I had quite a number of bits and pieces.
When I met Paul he was enthusiastic. He began to
translate them at once. We took them to Dagbladet
– Norweigan Daily newspaper. They accepted them
and so began a series that ran for nearly two years
under the title: "Profile of Famous Negroes." And
so in 1972, "Long Black Road" was born. Paul had

translated the book, designed the cover and painted the portraits.

I have always had the yen to write. From my early childhood, I composed poems and little ditties. No one had paid much attention until the night of my graduation from High School. My speech as president of the class was somewhat of a sensation in my community. In my travels in Europe, my writing gradually became more meaningful. I began to tell the story of my people and their contribution to the cultural life in the USA. I became grounded in the knowledge of the forms of Black Music – Spirituals, Worksongs, Folksongs, Ragtime, Blues, Jazz and Gospel etc.

By the time I settled in Norway, I had found my "niche". In my career I would tell the story of my people who were brought in chains as slaves to America. They were forced to help build a land. They worked the fields and built the roads. Their labour was free. After nearly 400 years they are still treated as second class citizens. I would tell this story in song. I knew that I would be poor. And I also knew that otherwise I would not be happy. My mother had instilled a proudness of origin in me. It was rooted deep in my consciousness. This proudness of origin was the driving force within me that forced me to realise that to bring a knowledge of Black Music, Folklore and Culture to Europe was much more important to the cause of my people than my singing of O don Fatale.

In 1960, I gave my first program on "The American Negro History from 1619 to the Present Time." in schools in Oslo.

I have tried diligently to help students and teachers with language, style and interpretation of Black Music. Sometimes they are "hard-headed" and will not listen, but I still try. I still hear some announce, "we shall sing a Negro Spiritual, 'That Lucky Old Sun'." Negro Spirituals are religious music. Sometimes Europeans and Americans get too "exotic and arty" in their rendition of Negro Spirituals, yet I know one must expect such treatment of Folk music.

Over the years, I have tried to explain the different forms in black music. Whenever individual students, groups of teachers have called or written to me for information on any phase of Black history, I always take the time to supply them with facts. I have read articles, pamphlets and books where writers have used material from "Long Black Road". For that I am happy. When I heard gospel singers or groups do a part of my repertoire, I feel elated. However, I must admit that when Radio and TV refuse to allow me to sing a Gospel program, I am irked. I am reminded of Langston Hughes who wrote, "They have taken my blues and gone."

I feel that my choice of program has been right. How many times have I read reviews and heard the comment, "there is something for every music taste in a Ruth Reese program, or R.R. in her unique way, or R.R., the artist with so many strings on which to play." That the public has been pleased with me is evident in the nearly always full-packed houses when I have sung.

All in all it has been a hard, challenging and exciting Underway. My ego was given a tremendous boost, when I opened ["Who's Who"] for 1984 and found Ruth Reese listed. And in June of 1984 the Oslo Community gave me one of its Cultural Prizes.

I am well aware of the fact that my political activity has hurt my singing career. Singing, I suppose, should be enough. Not for me. There are millions of poor human beings on this earth who do not have a chance to air their grievances. I believe artists, who have the ear of the public, should speak out for these unfortunate brothers and sisters.

I have tried, and will continue, to speak and sing for change. I have always cast my lot with the people. They have never let me down. And for that, I thank God.